EDEXCEL GCSE IN BUSINESS UNIT 1: INTRODUCTION TO SMALL BUSINESS

Ian Marcousé

Hodder Arnold
A MEMBER OF THE HODDER HEADLINE GROUP

Orders: please contact Bookpoint Ltd, 130 Milton Park, Abingdon, Oxon OX14 4SB. Telephone: (44) 01235 827720. Fax: (44) 01235 400454. Lines are open from 9.00–5.00, Monday to Saturday, with a 24-hour message answering service. You can also order through our website www.hodderheadline.co.uk

British Library Cataloguing in Publication Data
A catalogue record for this title is available from the British Library

ISBN 978 0 340 92697 0

First Published 2006
Impression number   10 9 8 7 6 5 4 3 2
Year   2012 2011 2010 2009 2008 2007

Copyright © 2006 Ian Marcousé

All rights reserved. No part of this publication may be reproduced or transmitted in any form or by any means, electronic or mechanical, including photocopy, recording, or any information storage and retrieval system, without permission in writing from the publisher or under license from the Copyright Licensing Agency Limited. Further details of such licenses (for reprographic reproduction) may be obtained from the Copyright Licensing Agency Limited, Saffron House, 6–10 Kirby Street, London EC1N 8TS.

Cover photo © Randy Faris/CORBIS
Typeset by GreenGate Publishing Services, Tonbridge, Kent
Illustrations by Barking Dog Art
Printed in Malaysia for Hodder Arnold, an imprint of Hodder Education and a member of the Hodder Headline Group, an Hachette Livre UK Company, 338 Euston Road, London NW1 3BH by Kim Hup Lee

Contents

Using this book v
Acknowledgements vi

Section 1: Spotting a Business Opportunity 1

1. An introduction to business enterprise 2
2. Understanding customer needs 6
3. Customer demand 10
4. Market mapping 15
5. Competition – role and limitations 18
6. Analysing competitor strengths and weaknesses 22
7. Understanding the need to add value 25
8. Invention and innovation 29
9. Assessing a franchise opportunity 33

Section 2: Showing Enterprise 39

10. Introduction to enterprise skills 40
11. Thinking creatively 44
12. Deliberate creativity 47
13. Business risks and rewards 51
14. Calculated risks 56
15. Other enterprise qualities 59

CONTENTS

Section 3: Putting a Business Idea into Practice — 65

16. Introduction to getting it right — 66
17. Estimating revenue — 71
18. Estimating costs — 75
19. Calculating and using profit — 80
20. The role and importance of cash — 84
21. Forecasting cash flow — 89
22. Raising finance — 93
23. Objectives when starting up — 99

Section 4: Making the Start-up Effective — 103

24. Introduction to effective start-up — 104
25. Customer focus and the marketing mix — 108
26. Is the customer always right? — 113
27. Limited versus unlimited liability — 116
28. Start-up legal and tax issues — 120
29. Effective, on-time delivery — 125
30. Recruiting the right staff — 129
31. Staff training — 133
32. Motivation — 138

Section 5: Understanding the Economic Context — 143

33. Introduction to the economic context — 144
34. Demand and supply — 149
35. Prices in commodity markets — 153
36. Interest rates — 158
37. Exchange rates — 162
38. Changes in economic activity — 167
39. Forecasting economic activity — 172
40. Stakeholders — 175
41. The effect of business and economic activity on stakeholders — 179

Tackling the on-screen exam — 185
What next? Moving on from Unit 1 — 187
Index — 189

Using this book

This book matches Unit 1 of the new Edexcel GCSE business course. Unit 1 is about the excitement and the challenges of starting and running a small business. The book focuses on exactly the same themes. It does it by using the real stories of dozens of different people starting up their own enterprises. Most are in business to make money, but the book also looks at why and how people start social enterprises such as charities.

The book is written to be read, not only under your teacher's direction, but for your own reading and understanding. Unit by unit, you follow the logic of starting up and running a business; yet each unit is self-contained, so if you want to read unit 13 before unit 12, that should not be a problem.

This new GCSE course has been designed to test your understanding of business more than your knowledge of facts, and this is the key to tackling the questions at the end of each unit. Do make sure to tackle the longer questions too. Your teacher might not ask you to do this every time, but it is sensible for you to read the exercises and think about how to answer them. Your teacher will probably have the answer book, and could let you have a copy of the mark scheme for any question you have done.

The book is full of business stories, many of which are very recent. It would be wonderful, though, if you also read up-to-date stories in the day's papers or in *Business Active* magazine. Your exam grades will be helped hugely by general knowledge of business. Try not to leave everything up to your teacher.

Please be aware that, towards the back of the book, are a couple of useful extra units:

- Tackling the on-screen exam
- What next? Moving on from Unit 1 (an explanation of the rest of the course, for those who are continuing beyond Unit 1 (the business short course).

May I wish you every success with this book and with the course.

Ian Marcousé, author of the book

Teachers

The book is accompanied by the *Teachers' Resource*, which includes answers to all the exercises. This is available from Hodder Arnold.

Acknowledgements

I owe a debt of gratitude to all my 2005/2006 GCSE business studies students at Lambeth College. They patiently read chapters and tackled questions. Special mentions go to Salma, Aaliyah, Angell and Yuli, who all made an extra effort to provide feedback. Many thanks are also due to Ian Rowbory, Andrew Ashwin, Nigel Watson and Sue Alpin for their help in devising the syllabus. At Hodder Arnold, the key figure was Alexia Chan. My thanks and best wishes to her.

Every effort has been made to trace and acknowledge ownership of copyright. The publishers will be glad to make suitable arrangements with any copyright holders whom it has not been possible to contact. The author and publishers would like to thank the following for the use of photographs in this volume:

Albert Ferreira/Rex Features, p7; Alex Segre/Rex Features, p36; APIX/Alamy, p166; Bang & Olufsen, p169; BMW Group, pp49, 145; Chris Radburn/PA/EMPICS, p18; CLARO CORTES IV/Reuters/Corbis, p181; Colin Shepherd/Rex Features, p47; DAMIAN DOVARGANES/AP/EMPICS, p31; David Pearson/Alamy, p128; Don Heiny/Corbis, p138; Doug Peters/allaction.co.uk/EMPICS, p112; Duncan Hale-Sutton/Alamy, p176; Dyson, p29; Fiona Hanson/PA/Topham, p42; Foodpix/photolibrary.com, p81; Francesco Guidicini/Rex Features, p104; Halo GB Ltd, p98; HLL, Hindustan Lever Limited, p9; Ian Leonard/Alamy, p131; Ian Miles Flashpoint Pictures/Alamy, p58; Innocent Drinks, p2; Jack Kurtz/The Image Works/topfoto.co.uk, p154; Jonathan Player/Rex Features, pp133, 148; Karl Prouse/topfoto.co.uk, p56; Mark Whitfield/Rex Features, p63; Mike Egerton/EMPICS, p61; Mike Egerton/EMPICS/Chelsea FC, p141; Mike Wilkinson/topfoto.co.uk, p175; www.morgueFile.com, p90; Mo Walker Photography, photographersdirect.com, p17; Najlah Feanny/Corbis, p156; PA/EMPICS, p88; Paul Bradforth/Alamy, p72; Phil Noble/ PA/EMPICS, p43; Phil Wilkinson/topfoto.co.uk, p95; Photodisc, p28; Rex Features, p23; Rui Vieira/PA/EMPICS, pp174, 179; Scenics & Science/Alamy, p167; Sebastien Bossi/Rex Features, p100; Sipa Press/Rex Features, p55; Steven May/Alamy, p162; StockShot/Alamy, p106; Tony Savino/The Image Works, p120; Topfoto.co.uk, p40; Topfoto, p66; Toru Hanai/Reuters/Corbis, p125; TSSA, p114.

This high quality material is endorsed by Edexcel and has been through a rigorous quality assurance programme to ensure that it is a suitable companion to the specification for both learners and teachers. This does not mean that its contents will be used verbatim when setting examinations nor is it to be read as being the official specification – a copy of which is avilable at www.edexcel.org.uk

SECTION 1

SPOTTING A BUSINESS OPPORTUNITY

1 An introduction to business enterprise

Business enterprise is about starting something of your own. It would most probably be a business, but it might be a charity, a pressure group or a sports club. The key is that *you* want to do it, and that it proves to be a success.

After several years of talking about it, three young university graduates started up **Innocent Drinks** in 1999. They wanted their own business, to be able to do things their own way. Now it is Britain's market leader in fruit smoothies, with annual sales of over £35 million. Londoners are used to seeing its vans painted like cows, with a horn that moos. Innocent staff get a £2000 bonus for having a baby and can apply for a £1000 bonus to do something they have always dreamed of, such as travelling to Peru. Pepsi would pay a fortune to buy the business (easily £100 million), but the three founders like things just the way they are.

There are three main questions to ask about start-up:

1 Why?
2 Who?
3 How?

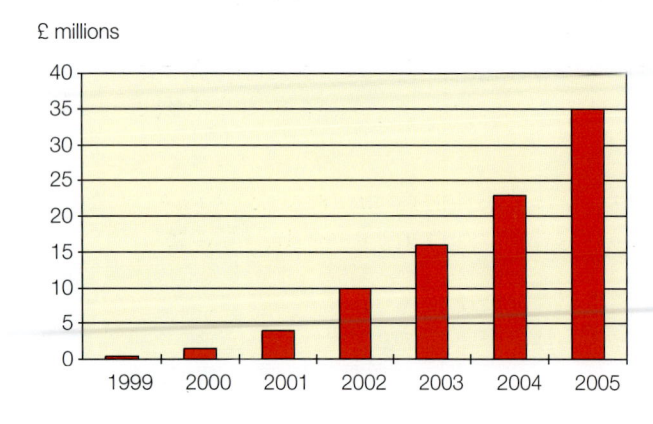

Annual sales, Innocent Drinks Ltd

Why?

> 'If you start off with a view to just making money, you'll probably make some, but you won't make a lot – you have to have a passion to succeed.'
>
> Howard Hodgson, businessman

- The main motive for starting up something new is desire. People want satisfaction from a sense of achievement. If they could get it from their normal workplace, they might not bother. Terry Leahy, chief executive of **Tesco**, has become wealthy, famous and powerful from a lifetime spent climbing the career ladder at one company. Many others find frustrations at work and want to break out, to give themselves a challenge.
- The next most important motivator is the wish to be your own boss. Independent decision making allows the individual to do things the way they think is best. Most jobs involve a degree of compromise. When you are running something for yourself you may not be able to afford the best, but at least you know that you will get the best you can afford. So the chef who hates working in a cramped kitchen with second-rate ingredients may long to be in a position to make all the decisions.
- Then, of course, there is money. A person may start a burger bar because of the conviction that it will make a fortune. Such a person may dream of retiring early, with a beachfront house and a huge fridge packed with beer. The typical business to go for would be a franchise, in which the individual buys the rights to open a local branch of a business that already exists (and makes good profits). The **Subway** sandwich chain works in this way.

Who?

> 'We can spend our whole lives underachieving.'
>
> Philip Crosby, quality guru

Successful start-up requires a huge list of qualities and skills, especially if starting up on your own. Among these are:

- personal qualities: determination; resilience (can bounce back from setbacks); enthusiasm; hard-working; decisive; willing to take risks
- skills: can listen as well as speak; can plan and organise; can persuade; can manage others
- resources: can find help when needed (finance or advice); may have exceptional knowledge of a special topic (e.g. building a website).

Of course, few entrepreneurs (business risk-takers) have *all* these qualities. But without quite a number of them, it will be hard to succeed.

How?

The most common way to start a new enterprise is to trial a business idea while still working, often from your own home. It is tried out in a limited way before committing too much money.

Unit 1 An introduction to business enterprise

SECTION 1 Spotting a business opportunity

> 'A man is a success if he gets up in the morning and gets to bed at night, and in between he does what he wants to do.'
>
> Bob Dylan, musician

Duncan Goose, however, started **One** water as a social enterprise by giving up his regular job. It took him six months, without pay, to get the enterprise going. (Water is bottled in Wales, sold throughout Britain and the profits go to a water charity based in Africa.) Duncan receives no pay from One, which he now runs three days a week, earning money during the other two days.

When people need to raise capital to help them start a business, they write a business plan. This sets out the aims, the plan, the financial forecasts and financial requirements. If carried out professionally, a good business plan greatly increases the chances of getting funding. Crucial to a good business plan is a sensible sales forecast, based on independent market research.

Exercises

(A and B: 25 marks; 30 minutes)

A Read the unit, then ask yourself:

1 Use the three points made under the heading 'Why?' to outline the motives of the graduates who started Innocent Drinks in 1999. (4)

2 Look at the bar chart on page 2. If Innocent Drinks' profit in 2005 was 20 per cent of its annual sales figure, how much profit did the business make? Show your workings. (3)

3 Explain why a younger person might prefer to start up a franchise rather than a wholly independent business. (4)

4 Without looking back at the text, briefly write down what you understand by the Why?, Who? and How? of starting a business. (4)

B Although 50 per cent of the working population are women, only 3.5 per cent of big business directors are women. And whereas 8 per cent of the UK population is non-white, only 1.5 per cent of big business directors are non-white. This may explain a huge amount of interest in business start-up among women and non-whites. Unfortunately, even then discrimination may apply. A recent survey showed that banks charge businesswomen a 1 per cent higher interest rate than businessmen.

1 Why might the figures 'explain a huge amount of interest in business start-up among women and non-whites'? (3)

2 How effective would you expect women to be at the business skills listed under the heading 'Who?' within the text? (3)

3 Outline two reasons why a bank might decide to charge businesswomen a higher rate of interest than men. (4)

Practice questions (15 marks; 20 minutes)

A social enterprise

Duncan Goose was chatting in a pub with friends about how to make the world a better place. The idea emerged of a not-for-profit bottled water, in which all the surplus from trading would go to charity. Later, Duncan stumbled across the South African charity Roundabout. In summer 2004 he gave up his job to work, unpaid, on One water.

In parts of Africa, women walk several miles to a well, hand-pumping the water into flasks or plastic bottles, and then carry it home. Roundabout is a charity that provides villages with (free) water pumps, powered by children's roundabouts! The kids' energy in pushing the roundabout pumps water into a water tower. Then people can simply draw the water from a tap, instead of having to pump it themselves.

The bottling plant started operating in spring 2005, and One started to be made available to shops in July. Now Duncan, who has been living on his savings since giving up his job, is trying to achieve distribution through enough shops to make the whole business work. Already he has been able to finance four water roundabouts.

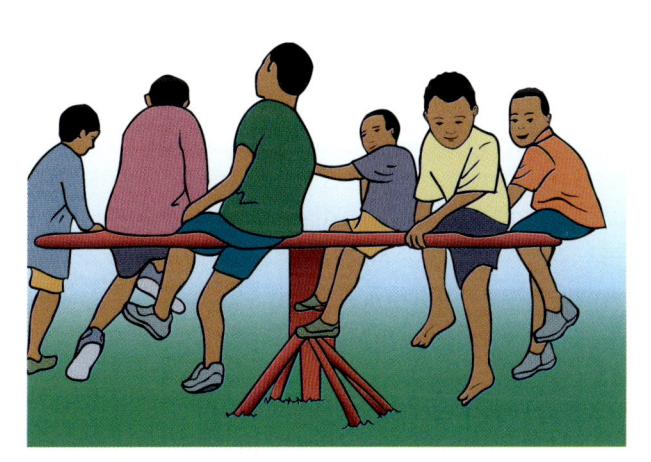

Questions

1 Outline three qualities and/or skills shown by Duncan in founding One. (6)
2 Explain Duncan's motives in founding One. (4)
3 Discuss how Duncan could try to persuade teenagers to buy One water instead of the more familiar brands, such as Evian and Highland Spring. (5)

2 Understanding customer needs

There are really only three ways to start up a successful business:

1. Do something really new (and that people want).
2. Do something that already exists, but do it better.
3. Do something that already exists, but at lower cost.

All three rely on learning what people want and what they need, then combining this with a full understanding of what existing businesses are supplying. Any gap between what people want and what they currently get gives rise to an opportunity. Unfortunately, many gaps that look significant prove very hard to fill. One example is banking. A recent survey showed that 10 million people were dissatisfied with their current high-street bank, yet few make a switch. Research might make a new bank account sound a winner, but customers might be too lazy to make the change.

For a microbusiness

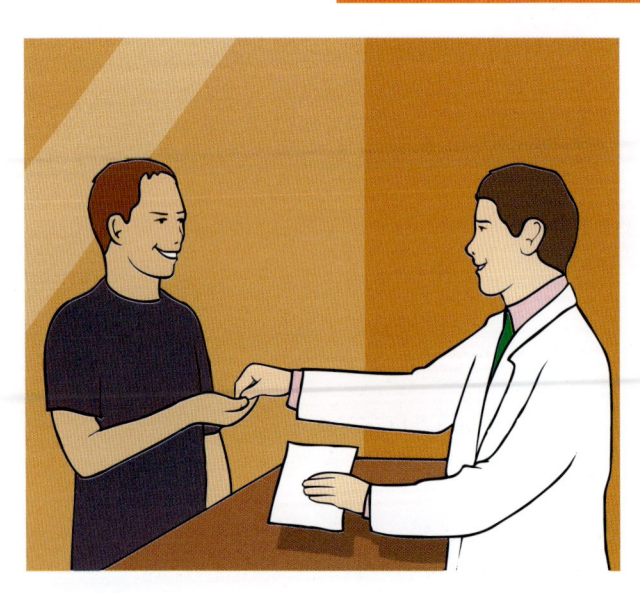

If the business is small, the owner does everything. S/he deals directly with customers and can therefore come to understand them fully. When prices rise, do customers notice, even grumble, or do they not really seem to care? The builder learns that customers get angrier about not sweeping up than serious building mistakes.

Yet plenty of small firms give poor service. There are bars where the staff are grumpy and shops that are dirty and messy. The bosses have forgotten that success comes from serving customers. At such places, the owner thinks that the world owes him or her a living;

Good customer service is the key to success

in fact, no business deserves to make a penny unless its staff are making an effort.

For a big business

> 'An industry begins with customer needs, not with a patent, a raw material or a selling skill.'
> Theodore Levitt, business thinker

Tesco plc has annual sales of £40 billion, with over 2000 stores, staffed by nearly 250,000 people. What chance is there that **Tesco** boss Terry Leahy will know all the customers' needs? In fact, he will know a great deal, because market research questionnaires will be recording what customers think and do. Beyond that, he will trust that local store managers understand their own area well enough to make good decisions. Part of Tesco's success has been that the company provides a wide range of products. The bargain-hungry shopper is satisfied, and so is the one looking for 'Tesco's Finest'. So Terry Leahy does not need to guess customer needs; he provides choice.

Do something really new

Jeff Bezos

In 1995 a 25-year-old borrowed some money from his parents and started **amazon.com**. Today, the world's biggest book retailer is worth billions of dollars, as are Jeff Bezos and his parents. Amazon was the first internet retailer; Bezos saw an opportunity before anyone else and built up the business at an amazing speed, making it impossible for anyone to catch up. Above all else, though, he recognised that certain customers need to be able to buy books online because they have no bookshop nearby. (Like all great business ideas, it seems very obvious now, looking back.) Among other great examples of doing something really new (in their day) are:

- Maltesers, first launched in 1936
- KitKat, first launched in 1937
- the Mini, first driven in 1959
- Sky TV, first shown in the late 1980s.

Do something that already exists, but do it better

> 'Find out what she doesn't know she wants.'
> A well-known saying at the US giant company, Procter & Gamble

Many companies have succeeded hugely with this approach. The American company Procter & Gamble is famous for it. It spent six years developing the **Pringles** potato crisp – making sure the taste, crispness and packaging were just right. (The company likes to say, 'It's better to be right than to be first.')

The company that is first has many advantages, but the company that arrives later has the chance to research carefully into what customers really want. **PlayStation** came after the Nintendo console,

Unit 2 Understanding customer needs

SECTION 1 Spotting a business opportunity

but came to dominate; Sainsbury's was Britain's first middle-class supermarket, but Tesco stole its market.

Do something that already exists, but at lower cost

> 'The key to success for Sony, and to everything in business, science and technology is never to follow the others.'
>
> Masaru Ibuka, co-founder of Sony

People think it is easy to make money by cutting prices. In fact, it is very easy to lose money doing that. Sales may jump, but tiny profits per unit sold combine with huge stresses from selling more. You need more sales staff, more security guards, more floor space, and so on. After buying Safeway in 2004, **Morrisons** cut prices dramatically at the Safeway shops. Sales rose, but profits collapsed.

The really clever companies are those, like **Ryanair**, that do not begin by cutting prices. They start by cutting costs. Ryanair cut out free food and drinks, then cut the time it takes to clean, refuel and reload the planes. Then they cut all payments to travel agents (passengers book online). Only then, when its costs were low, did Ryanair start to cut prices – and they kept cutting. For the first time, in August 2005, Ryanair flew more passengers than British Airways.

Exercises

(A and B: 25 marks; 30 minutes)

A Read the unit, then ask yourself:

1 Explain why the boss of a small firm should find it easier to understand customer needs than the boss of a big firm. (3)
2 Outline two advantages to a firm of coming up with something really new, such as Maltesers (back in 1936). (4)
3 What problem might be caused for a firm that tries to improve profits by cutting prices? (2)
4 Outline the customer need that was met by:
   a) McDonald's, started in America in 1954 (2)
   b) the teabag, first manufactured by Lipton in 1952 (2)
   c) Phones4U, started in 1996. (2)

B On 29 June 2005 Sony announced the closure of one of its South Wales factories, with the loss of 650 jobs. The company explained that demand had slumped for 'fat telly' production, with flat screens accounting for 70 per cent of sales in Europe in 2005. These are produced by Sony in Spain. Sony was slow to see the customer demand for flat-screen TVs. Samsung dominates this relatively new sector.

1 Outline two ways in which Sony's managers should have known about customers' preference for flat-screen TVs. (4)
2 Do you think it is inevitable that factory workers suffer for the mistakes made by managers? (3)
3 Samsung outfought Sony by going for 'something really new' – the flat-screen TV. How might Sony respond in future? (3)

Practice questions (20 marks; 25 minutes)

Safe water – needed by 1000 million 'customers'

The Indian branch of Unilever has come up with a new product designed to meet a real local need – for pure water. In India 400,000 people a year die from contaminated water. Families are advised to boil the water for 20 minutes, then let it cool. The fuel cost (and extra heat and time) means that many reject this option. They take their chances.

Unilever India has spent five years developing Pureit, a purifier that can clean any water, making it fresh and keeping it fresh. You can pour polluted water in the top and draw fresh, clean water from the bottom. Pureit was launched in February 2005 at a price of £20. By the end of May it had achieved its target of 40,000 units. Clearly the scope for sales growth is vast, with perhaps 100 million households in India that could benefit from Pureit. The World Health Organization says that 1000 million people have unsafe drinking water, but the grim commercial fact is that many of these will have too low an income level to afford Unilever's new product.

A customer need is not enough. For businesses, the need only matters if it is backed by the ability to pay.

The Pureit water purifier

Questions

1 Unilever has identified a life-and-death need. Explain why it may be hard for the company to make it profitable. (4)
2 What might be the impact on Unilever staff if the business decided to go ahead with selling Pureit, even if it did not seem likely to be profitable? (6)
3 Is it right to profit from people's desperation to obtain safe drinking water? Discuss. (10)

3 Customer demand

> 'You can hype a questionable product for a little while, but you'll never build an enduring business.'
>
> Victor Kiam, chief executive, Remington

Demand is the quantity of a product that customers want to buy. Of course, we may all *want* a brand new BMW, but not be able to afford one. For demand to be meaningful, it has to be backed up by the ability to pay. This is known as **effective demand**.

Demand for bottles of Danone's brand **Actimel** depends on a number of factors:

1. The price of Actimel.
2. The price of rival brands, such as Yakult.
3. Fashion and taste. (Are consumers trying to spend money on their health?)
4. How easy is it to find and buy? (Distribution and display)
5. How well promoted is it? (The level and quality of advertising spending)

The price

The price of a product or service is a key influence on the level of demand. Occasionally a company may charge too low a price; customers may lose confidence and go elsewhere. A wedding dress for £99.99 might not win hearts and minds.

In the vast majority of cases, higher prices push demand down. A price increase for **Pepsi** would cut demand, especially if it made it more expensive than **Coke**. Price increases encourage customers to look for cheaper substitutes; and also may push products out of people's price range. As the graph shows, not all Chelsea supporters have a high enough income to spend £800+ on a season ticket. So the **demand curve** slopes downwards: the higher the price, the lower the demand.

Demand for Chelsea season tickets

The price of rival brands

Although a Chelsea supporter would not switch to Crystal Palace just because of cheaper tickets, sales of *The Times* newspaper doubled between 1995 and 2005. During that whole period the price of *The Times* was cut far below that of its main rivals. So even if you leave your own price the same, sales could suffer because of a cut in the price of rival products or services.

Fashion and taste

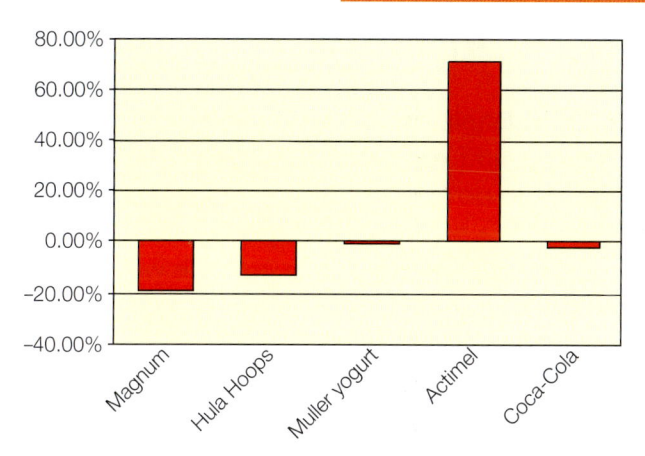

% sales change 2004 compared with 2003
(Source: AC Nielsen Top 100 Grocery Brands)

In 2001, four years after it launched in Britain, Actimel had sales of under £25 million. By 2005 sales reached £125 million. British households had become concerned about organic food and the contents of school dinners. Actimel's challenge to drink a little pot of 'probiotic' yoghurt fitted in. Instead of worrying about what to eat and drink, here was an apparently 'good' food. While products such as Wall's Magnum and Coca-Cola were struggling, Actimel was at the height of food fashion.

How easy is it to find and buy?

Small new brands from small producers can find it very hard to gain shelf space. Supermarkets stock thousands of profitable products, and are unlikely to take a profit-maker off the shelf to test out a newcomer. Major producers such as Danone (Actimel) or Müller (Vitality) have no such problem. Retailers such as Tesco are willing to test out new things, especially if there is the promise that the new product will be backed by extensive advertising.

How well promoted is it?

> 'Brand loyalty is very much like an onion. It has layers and a core. The core is the user who will stick by your brand until the very end.'
> Chief executive, Procter & Gamble

Three forms of promotion prove the most important:

1. Packaging gives the opportunity to create an image and help repeat-purchasers to find the product next time.
2. Advertising is the other image creator. Actimel has been styled as a product for young, active adults who want to boost their health and their enjoyment of life.
3. Sales promotion can boost short-term sales (e.g. offering trial packs at special prices).

> 'Profit in business comes from repeat customers, customers that boast about your product and service, and that bring friends with them.'
> W. Edwards Deming, business guru

In addition to the quality of promotion comes the quantity. In 2001 Danone spent £8 million advertising Actimel, at a time when sales were only £24 million. So one third of the sales revenue was spent on advertising, which was a remarkably heavy investment in the brand.

For individual products, other important influences on demand include:

- seasonality (e.g. toys in December and sunscreens in July and August)
- the weather: umbrellas, ice creams, roofing and fencing (sales of the latter jump after high winds).

Product trial and repeat purchase

Demand is a function of getting people to try, then getting them to stay. In other words, product trial and **repeat purchase**. In most cases, advertising is the method to obtain trial, with the qualities of the product being relied on to achieve a high level of repeat purchase. The weakness of this approach is that advertising is an expensive way to get customers to try; and there is a risk of losing them if the image is not right for repeat purchase.

Many new products flop when people drift away once the advertising stops. Producers have to make their brands strong enough to keep selling, even when advertising drops back. This has proved true for the Mars product **Celebrations** (sales are stable at about £75 million a year), though many other chocolate products struggle to keep selling beyond the trial stage.

Achieving repeat purchase requires not only a good quality product, but also distinctiveness. In other words, the product needs to stand out. **Tango** is a good quality sparkling orange drink, but unless it is advertised heavily, customers drift back to **Fanta**. Producers of toilet tissue suffer the same problem when up against **Andrex**, the dominant brand.

Products such as cars and wedding dresses are bought infrequently – so repeat purchase is less important. For lower-priced, frequent purchases, such as chocolate bars or toilet rolls, long-term success relies hugely on brand loyalty and therefore repeat business.

Successful products need to stand out

Revision essentials
Demand curve: the downward sloping line drawn to show how falling prices lead to rising sales (the 'curve' may be a straight line).
Effective demand: demand backed by the ability to pay.
Repeat purchase: customer loyalty reflected in regular purchasing.

Exercises

(A and B: 30 marks; 35 minutes)

A Read the unit, then ask yourself:

1 Explain why demand might not be effective. (3)

2 a) Draw a demand curve using this data for airline tickets from Manchester to Barcelona. (5)

Price	Demand (passengers per flight)
£140	55
£120	80
£100	105
£80	130
£60	155
£40	180

b) Calculate how much money would be generated by charging £140 per ticket. (2)

c) Calculate the selling price that generates the most money per flight. (4)

3 Identify two ways to improve the rate of repeat purchase for:
   a) L'Oréal hair colour products (2)
   b) Sony PlayStation software. (2)

B Each year Mars sells more than £125 million worth of Maltesers in Britain. The brand is 70 years old, but sales are still rising! The product is quite successful in other countries, but the British are the biggest Maltesers-eaters by far. Sales of Maltesers are more than twice those of Cadbury Flake.

1 Which two factors do you think are the main reasons for the high demand for Maltesers in Britain? Explain your reasons for each factor. (6)

2 Explain how Cadbury might try to boost sales of Flake:
   a) over the next month (3)
   b) over the next two to three years. (3)

Unit 3 Customer demand

Practice questions

(25 marks; 25 minutes)

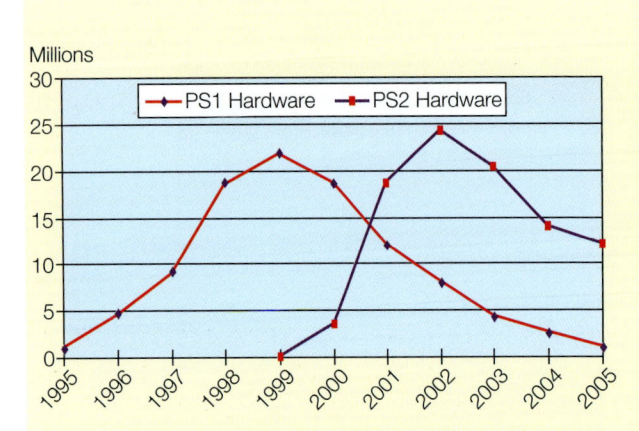

Life cycle of Sony Playstation 1 and 2 (note: these are accurately sourced figures for annual sales volumes for PS1 and PS2.)

Between the launch of the first PlayStation in 1995 and 2005, Sony dominated computer games. The PS2 sold 95 million consoles, compared with just 22 million for the Microsoft Xbox. The November 2005 launch of the Xbox 360, however, threatened to change everything. Sony was facing a serious challenge from the world's richest company.

The demand for games consoles has been huge, and profitable. But the big money is made by selling games. Even in 2001, six years after it was launched, PlayStation 1 sold 160 million games (worth around £3000 million). Now Sony's income from games is threatened because Xbox 360 launched six months before the Sony PS3 in 2006. In the games business, being first is an important factor in sales success.

Questions

1. Explain the likely impact of seasonality on sales of games consoles such as PS3. (3)

2. 'Every boy in America wants a PlayStation this Christmas', said a Sony website in the 1990s. What might stop that demand turning into sales? (3)

3. a) Look carefully at the graph. In their peak sales years, how many extra PS2s were sold compared with PS1s? Show your workings. (3)

    b) In 2004/5 Sony launched the portable PSP. Outline the evidence from the text and graph that Sony should really have been launching the PS3 at that time. (6)

4. Discuss whether the Xbox 360 or the PS3 is more likely to succeed over the coming years. (10)

4 Market mapping

Years ago, the secret to business success was price competition. Spot a successful business, copy its idea and offer the same thing, but cheaper. **Pepsi** did this with **Coke**; **Wrangler** did it with **Levi's**; and supermarkets do it all the time with own-label versions of new products.

To a certain extent it still happens, but within a careful attempt at mapping the market. This means setting out the key features of the market on a diagram, then plotting where each brand fits in. For example, in the chocolate market, key features include:

- luxury versus everyday eating (e.g. Flake versus Dairy Milk)
- filling versus light (e.g. Snickers versus Maltesers).

A **market map** based on this idea would look like the diagram below.

A business such as **Cadbury** would spend a substantial sum each year (perhaps £100,000) gaining the **market research** evidence to get this market map right. In other words, it would usually be based on the opinions of thousands of customers. Armed with this information, a decision could be taken, such as to work on a new product that has a luxury feel *and* is filling. In the recent past, Cadbury has tried a praline chocolate bar to fill this gap in the market; but no one has launched a brand successfully.

The idea of market mapping is to identify gaps, to show where a sector is overcrowded, and to stop a producer becoming over-reliant on one sector. **Mars** is very strong in the filling, everyday sector (Twix, Mars and Snickers), but this is a declining sector, as people worry about their weight. So the 1990s launch by Mars of **Celebrations** was a very clever move.

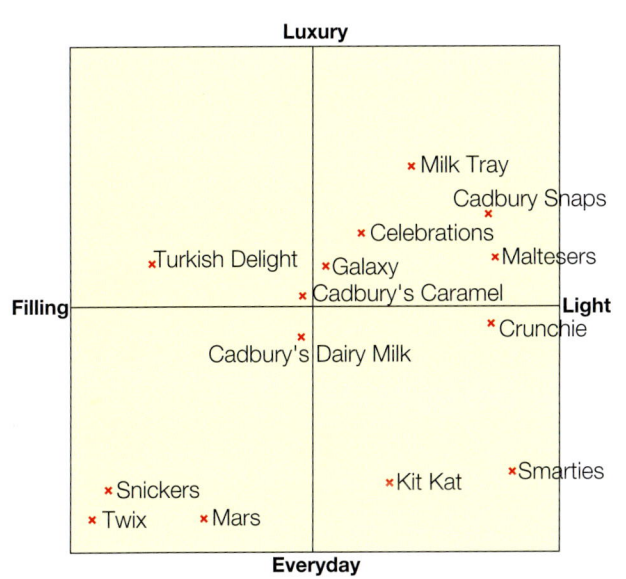

Source: author's estimates

Chocolate market map

For most businesses, the difficulty is in identifying the key factors to use in the mapping exercise. These might include:

- high-priced/low-priced;
- for the young/for the old;
- modern/traditional;
- for men/for women.

Companies decide on the 'right' factors after careful market research. Talking to customers may show that young and old have similar views about chocolate, whereas men and women think differently.

Market mapping is also very useful for a new small business, for example in building services. A good look through the *Thomson Local* directory may show lots of emergency plumbers, but few offering to fit luxury bathroom suites.

Of course, there remains a potential problem. Perhaps there is a gap because there is no effective demand locally. So further market research may need to be carried out. The fact that market mapping is not a magic solution should not stop it being used. All business decisions require thought; no single method provides guaranteed success.

> **Revision essentials**
> **Market map:** a grid that measures two different aspects of the brands within a market (e.g. young/old compared with luxury/economy).
> **Market research:** finding out customer opinions and actions, usually by interviews and by gathering information about sales.

Exercises

(A and B: 20 marks; 25 minutes)

A Read the unit, then ask yourself:

1 Suggest two reasons why it may no longer be enough to produce cheaper copies of product ideas. (2)
2 Explain why it suggests in the text that 'the 1990s launch by Mars of Celebrations was a very clever move'. (3)
3 a) Look carefully at the chocolate market map. Identify two possible market opportunities for a new company entering the market. (2)
    b) For one of those market opportunities, outline a product that you think might appeal to consumers. Suggest a price that you think would be appropriate. (5)

B For her recent GCSE project, Aliesha drew up a market map of her local area (Brixton, South London). She identified that there were many takeaways and cafes offering Caribbean food, but nowhere offering a smarter restaurant for special occasions. Her market research showed that 32 per cent of adults locally thought they would go to a smart Caribbean restaurant at least once a year. Aliesha was able to show that this business could be very profitable.

1. Outline one way in which Aliesha might have carried out her market research. (3)
2. Construct a market map for takeaways and fast-food outlets in your local area. Use as the scales: 1. expensive–cheap; 2. for young people–for older people. (5)

Unit 4 Market mapping

Practice questions

(20 marks; 25 minutes)

Between 2004 and 2006 the market for soft drinks has been transformed. In the past, soft drinks were targeted mainly at children. Fizzy drinks dominated, especially colas and lemonades. Huge social transformations have changed that. The big sales successes of recent years have been:

- Probiotic drinks, such as Yakult and Actimel.
- Red Bull and other energy drinks.
- Fruit smoothies, selling at £1.50 to £2 for a small bottle.
- Bottled water, especially brands such as Evian.

The market for colas remains huge – especially for diet varieties – but the rising stars are more adult-orientated. The soft drinks market map shows that although there are thousands of brands, there still seem to be large gaps.

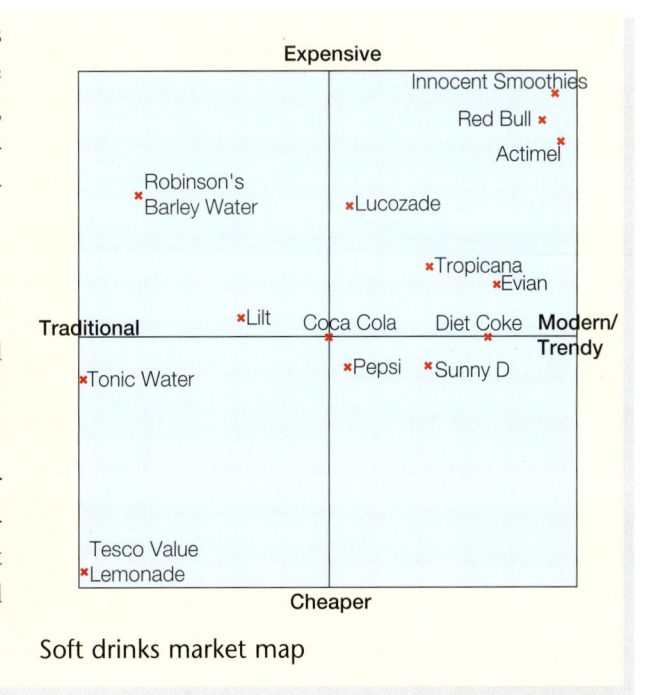

Soft drinks market map

Questions

1 a) Explain two benefits a soft drinks firm might gain from studying a market map. (4)

b) In this case, outline two conclusions Coca-Cola might reach from the soft drinks market map. (4)

2 Suggest two reasons why adults may be more interested in soft drinks nowadays. (4)

3 Discuss how a company might deal with a brand for which sales are falling, such as Lucozade. (8)

17

5 Competition – role and limitations

In 1981, when you moved into a new house you did not phone everyone to tell them. You did not have a phone. You applied to British Telecom (BT) to get a line for a phone. It took between one and three months. Within five years the position was transformed. For the first time, the government allowed competitors to enter the market for phones. BT quickly responded by speeding up their services and increasing choice. The arrival of competition improved things for the customer.

Competition is often the biggest headache for a new, small business. The business may identify a profitable market gap, but what if another firm arrives at the same time as you? Instead of being the only Thai restaurant in the village, there may be two – both half empty. Even if you get there first, your success may simply attract copycats.

This is why starting a business requires self-confidence and a willingness to take risks. Competitors may arrive early, making it very difficult, but they may not. It took **British Airways** four years to respond to **easyJet**'s introduction of online booking for aircraft seats. In the meantime easyJet built up its profitability so that price-cutting by British Airways was no longer a serious threat.

> *'Competition generates energy, rewards winners and punishes losers. It is therefore the fuel for the economy.'*
> Charles Handy, business guru

Benefits of competition to consumers

Benefits include:

- firms are forced to offer good products and a good service
- firms are forced to keep prices down
- in order to break away from fierce price competition, firms will try to bring in new, **innovative** products or services.

These consumer benefits place firms under constant pressure. A bright new idea will soon be copied by rivals. A profitable service may be undermined by price-cutting. This is clearly the case in businesses such as pizza delivery, where one firm's 'buy one get one free' is quickly matched by rival offers.

The pressure itself is a good thing. It stops anyone getting complacent. If a football team is so wealthy and dominant that it wins matches and trophies without playing well, the outcome is bad for everyone.

Drawbacks to competition

> *'Competition brings out the best in products and the worst in people.'*
> David Sarnoff, former president, RCA

Competition can force businesses to do things they would prefer to avoid. With high rents, city-centre bars have to get good trade on Fridays and Saturdays. If your rivals have special deals or 'drink as much as you like for £10' offers, you join in or close down. Similarly, if other banks have relocated their customer call centres to India, you may feel that you have to cut your own bank's costs by following them.

Fierce competition may force firms to:

- cut costs by cutting staff – bad for the staff and perhaps bad for customers
- take short-term action, such as price-cutting, that may damage the long-term health of the business
- adopt **unethical** practices, such as dumping waste materials or injecting water into meat (bacon often has 15 per cent extra water pumped into it, to make it easier to charge a price that customers think is good value for money).

Barriers to effective competition

Collusion

> *'People of the same trade seldom meet together, even for merriment and diversion, but the conversation ends in a conspiracy against the public, or in some contrivance to raise prices.'*
> Adam Smith, The Wealth of Nations, 1776

In some markets, producers may come to private agreements that prevent proper competition. This is quite common in the supply of big, bulky materials that cannot easily be imported from far away, such as cement or bulk chemicals. This **collusion** between producers is illegal, but successful prosecutions show that it does happen. The effect of collusion is to push prices up, perhaps creating unhealthily high profits among the firms concerned. A further risk is that the attempt to keep this secret may lead to corrupt practices such as bribery.

Subsidy

Governments may help their own firms at the expense of those from overseas. British farmers are able to buy 'red diesel', which carries no fuel duty. So whereas most of us pay perhaps £1 a litre for diesel, farmers pay around 30p. This subsidises them in competition with farmers from overseas, including those from very poor developing countries. It makes it harder for African farmers to compete with those from Britain.

Where markets are highly competitive, small firms have to look carefully for market gaps. It is too difficult to compete with **Tesco** and **Sainsbury's** in their main market; but there may be room for a small shop that sells only organic groceries, for example.

> **Revision essentials**
> **Collusion:** two or more firms agree to act together against the interests of customers.
> **Innovative:** a new, perhaps original, product or process.
> **Unethical:** an action or decision that is wrong from a moral standpoint.

Exercises

(A and B: 25 marks; 30 minutes)

A Read the unit, then ask yourself:

1. Identify two methods a new business might use to break into a competitive market. (2)
2. **a)** Explain why shoppers might benefit if a new supermarket chain arrived to challenge Tesco's number one position in the UK. (4)
   b) Outline two possible drawbacks to Tesco's shop-floor staff if a fierce competitor arrived. (4)
3. **a)** Why might it be unethical for a bar to run an offer such as 'drink as much as you like for £10'? (3)
   b) Why might competition force a bar to run such an offer anyway? (3)

B EU charges chemical firms with price-fixing

22 August 2005

BRUSSELS (Reuters) – A number of European chemicals firms have been charged with running a cartel for years to fix prices on chemicals that are used to make transparent plastics, used in cars, electronics and other consumer goods.

Four companies acknowledged they were charged, including Britain's Imperial Chemical Industries, the German companies Degussa and BASF and privately held British firm Lucite.

The European Commission charged the companies with fixing prices, allocating customers and passing on the additional costs. One source familiar with the situation said more than a dozen are involved.

(Source: uk.news.yahoo.com)

1 Why may these firms have decided to avoid acting as true competitors? (3)
2 How might the staff of the companies be affected by this collusion? (3)
3 How does the situation in the article compare with the quote given in the text from the famous economist Adam Smith? (3)

Practice questions

(20 marks; 25 minutes)

In May 2004 Wizz Air flew its first flight from Poland to London. Based upon the ideas of Ryanair and easyJet, it was Central and Eastern Europe's first low-cost airline. Cleverly financed, it operates new Airbus planes, but to secondary airports such as Luton and Liverpool rather than Heathrow or Manchester.

Within 11 months Wizz had flown 1 million passengers and by September 2005 the figure was up to 2 million. Wizz operates very full aircraft and is already profitable (it ordered 12 new planes in August 2005). If you want a trip to (beautiful) Budapest, it will cost about £3.20 one way, as long as you book a few months ahead. When booking only a day or two ahead, the price is more like £75.

Wizz has had an immediate impact upon airlines such as British Airways and the Polish airline LOT. Before Wizz, a late-booked return trip from London to Warsaw cost over £500. Today LOT charges £290 – but it would be £150 on Wizz.

(Source: www.wizzair.com)

Questions

1 Outline three ways travellers to Poland could benefit from the arrival of Wizz Air. (6)
2 In the short term Wizz is succeeding because it is the only substantial low-cost airline in Central and Eastern Europe. Outline two problems it may face when new airlines open up. (4)
3 a) It took 11 months for Wizz to fly its first million passengers and just 6 months for its second million. Identify three things that may have led to this rise in sales. (3)
   b) Discuss whether it would be unethical for Wizz to deliberately undercut the prices of LOT, with the intention of driving LOT out of business. (7)

6 Analysing competitor strengths and weaknesses

To start a business successfully you need to know where and how to fit into the market. In 2005 any business trying to launch an MP3 player had to acknowledge that **iPod** held the centre of the market. Its mixture of 'cool' and 'must-have' gave it a 70 per cent **market share**. For a new company, the strength of the iPod meant either giving up or finding small weaknesses that could provide small opportunities. For a new, small business, as for **Sony** or **Samsung**, the starting point was to look carefully at the iPod.

Analysing something means breaking it down into its component parts. Yes, iPod users love their iPods; but do they like everything about them? And what if the same person has an iPod and a **Nokia** and a Sony **PSP**? They might love them all, but find it irritating to carry them all round at the same time. So it is vital to study the strengths and weaknesses of competitors.

How to carry out the analysis

There are three ways to analyse the competition.

1. Customer research.
2. Retailer research.
3. Breaking the product/service down.

Customer research

Get groups of consumers talking about how, when and why they use the rival product or service; what exactly their experience has been, before and after buying; and whether they would buy the same thing again – and if not, why not? Before Sammi Garnett started up an Italian restaurant in Northampton, she and her boyfriend simply asked around at pubs in the town for views of the existing places to eat. She learnt that nowhere offered a good

Customer research

deal for office parties of eight of more people, and chose to make that a feature of her restaurant. It proved very successful, providing 25 per cent of all her business.

Retailer research

Your competitors may be loved by the public, but hated by the trade (i.e. the wholesalers and retailers who distribute the product). The supplier of Indian ready meals to **Morrisons** may sometimes deliver late or send the wrong quantities. This could be a golden opportunity to break into a market. So a food producer may decide to change its plan for a new range of Italian meals, and focus on Indian instead.

Breaking the product/service down

When a new iPod is launched, the first buyer is likely to be the big rival, Sony. Its engineers take the iPod apart to identify exactly what is inside and to analyse how the product has been made. They want to know if a corner has been cut, creating some possibility that Sony could offer better sound or faster downloading. James Dyson started his huge business by taking apart a Hoover vacuum cleaner and seeing that he could come up with a better way to sweep carpets.

What conclusions can be drawn?

To start up successfully, you need to know as much as possible about the market, the customers and the competitors. Having done that, you can make some decisions. **Ferrero** is a huge chocolate producer in Italy (and has worldwide brand successes such as Tic Tacs, Ferrero Rocher and Nutella chocolate spread). Its company motto is 'Be unique. Never copy.' When it came to Britain it assessed the strength of **Cadbury** and decided not to fight it. Instead it launched brands such as the Kinder Egg, Kinder Bueno and, of course, Ferrero Rocher. They are all successful, but none of them offers straightforward chocolate – because that is Cadbury's strength.

So Ferrero decided to avoid head-on competition. It found ways to appeal to **market segments**, such as children. In other cases, the decision may lead to a much more direct approach. Anyone analysing the UK market for women's clothing between 1995 and 2005 has spotted weaknesses at **Marks and Spencer**. Some, such as **Matalan** and **Primark**, decided prices were far too high. Others, such as **Zara** and **Topshop**, decided the clothes were too old-fashioned, and that M&S reacted far too slowly to fashion changes. So both developed an approach based upon speed: quickly turning new catwalk styles into ready-to-buy clothes.

For a new business starting up locally, careful analysis of the local competition is a must. If the rivals are all really strong, you may decide not to start up at all. Unless you know how you can be better, you should not risk your money. Usually, though, businesses are far from perfect. The small grocer may be cramped and unfriendly. The cinema may have one screen and be uncomfortable. If you can build your strength on your competitor's weakness, the result should be successful.

> **Revision essentials**
> **Market segments:** sections of a market focused upon specific types of customer, such as children.
> **Market share:** one brand's sales as a percentage of all the sales in the market.

Exercises (20 marks; 25 minutes)

Read the unit, then ask yourself:

1 Outline two business benefits from holding a 70 per cent share of a market. (4)
2 If you were about to start up a business selling packets of home-made fudge, what might you learn from retailer research? Outline two ideas. (4)
3 Discuss the value of Ferrero's motto ('Be unique. Never copy.') when competing with other firms. (6)
4 Explain why a large firm such as Ferrero might decide to avoid head-on competition with another large firm such as Cadbury. (6)

Practice questions (20 marks; 25 minutes)

In August 2005 Sam Harrison opened Sam's Brasserie and Bar in Chiswick, West London. He had been working on plans to start his own business for two years, since returning to England from two years at the Bondi Beach Cafe in Australia.

Sam's idea for a restaurant came from looking at the competition. All the high-quality restaurants in West London offered lunch and dinner at tightly set times, such as 12.30–2.00 and 7.00–11.00. Sam believed that many people want to eat at whatever time suits them, therefore his restaurant is open from 9.00 a.m. to 11.00 p.m. The style is relaxed, so people come and go when they want to.

This idea is proving a great success. Within a month of opening, customer numbers are 1000 a week, with an average spend of £35 per person. This revenue is much higher than expected, which should mean that the business moves into profit quickly. (Source: adapted from *Caterer and Hotelkeeper*, 22–28 September 2005)

Questions

1 a) Explain the weakness that Sam identified among his competitors. (3)
   b) How did his plans turn this weakness into a strength for his own business? (3)
2 Sam says that 'we need to continue to build this business and work hard to keep the customers coming'. Outline three factors that are likely to be important for Sam's Brasserie to keep getting repeat business. (6)
3 a) If sales continue at the rate mentioned in the text, what will be the annual revenue from Sam's first year in business? (3)
   b) Outline the costs that Sam will have to allow for before he can calculate the profit generated by the business. (5)

7 Understanding the need to add value

'The real issue is value, not price.'
Robert Lindgren, Harvard Business Review

Many shops sell **Walkers** crisps at 35p per pack. The pack weighs 30g, which is about 1p of potatoes. In the pack is oil, salt and flavouring, but even adding in the cost of the packaging, the total cost per unit could not be more than 3p. So turning potatoes into crisps adds value. It 'creates' value by making the customer willing to pay extra. In the case of crisps, turning 3p into 35p adds 1100 per cent to the value of the potato (33/3 × 100). That's good business.

Is **adding value** a rip-off? Not necessarily. A sandwich sold for £1.50 may contain ingredients costing 40p. So the baker is receiving £1.10 for two slices of bread. Assuming 20 slices in a loaf, that's selling a loaf of bread for £11 instead of £1. Yet when people are going out, they do not want to have to take butter, cheese, tomato and a knife with them. They would rather buy a sandwich. They are happy to pay for speed and convenience.

'What we obtain too cheap we esteem too little; it is dearness only that gives everything its value.'
Thomas Paine, eighteenth-century political thinker

A sandwich is more than its ingredients – it has added value

How to add value

Added value is the difference between the cost of materials and the selling price. Value can be added either by pushing the price up or by cutting the costs. Usually it is by adding in a feature that makes the item more valuable to the customer. That enables the price to be increased.

Different ways to make the item more valuable to the customer are:

- **convenience and speed:** in Britain, most people will pay extra to save their own time, as shown in the table below

Adding value by adding convenience

Chicken curry and rice	Price per person (£)
Cook your own	1.00
Add Sharwood's bottle sauce to chicken	1.25
Buy supermarket ready meal	2.50
Buy takeaway	3.50
Go to restaurant	4.75

- **good design:** a beautifully designed dress might sell for £200, while one using exactly the same quantity of material might sell for just £20
- **high quality manufacture or service:** a Lexus sells at £50,000 because it is regarded as one of the best-made cars in the world; it never breaks down and is like sitting in a huge leather armchair
- **the brand name:** a Nike swoosh adds tens of pounds to the 'value' of a pair of trainers; a Mercedes badge on the front of a car adds thousands of pounds to the value of a new car; cleverly, the 1997 start-up of Innocent Drinks quickly established this brand name as an indication of quality, freshness and originality
- **a unique feature:** a USP, or **unique selling point** is something that makes the product worth paying extra for (e.g. a family car with flat-screen TVs and headphones in the back of the front passenger seats).

The importance of value added

People starting businesses often forget about the everyday costs. There are obvious ones such as electricity and phones, but also others such as the cost of 'wastage' (theft plus damaged goods), or the cost of recruiting and training new staff. All these costs have to be paid for out of the value added. So there needs to be a big enough difference between price and bought-in costs to allow internal costs to be paid for. The fashion clothing company **Ted Baker** adds £62 million of value to its £43 million of bought-in costs (such as clothes made by outside suppliers). The diagram shows that the shareholders receive £5 million of the value added; the rest is spent within the business or paid in tax to the government.

> *'Consumers buy products, but they choose brands.'*
> Procter & Gamble saying, from 'P&G 99'

SECTION 1 Spotting a business opportunity

Income £105m

Value added £62m

Bought-in costs £43m

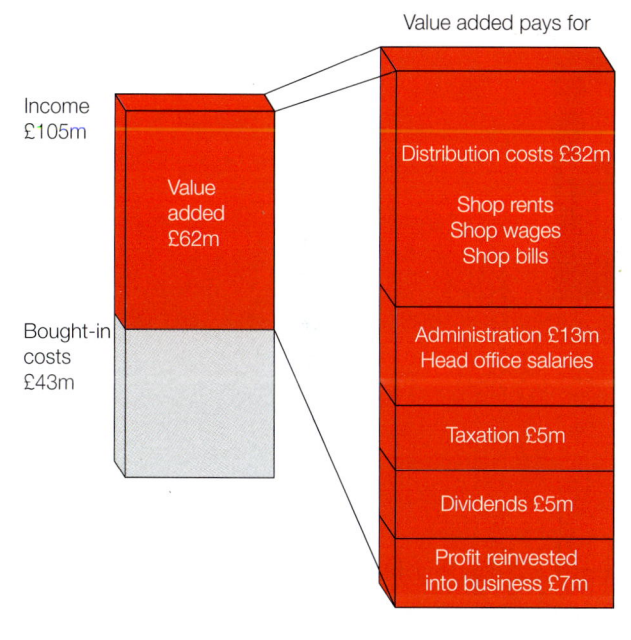

Value added pays for:
- Distribution costs £32m
- Shop rents, Shop wages, Shop bills
- Administration £13m, Head office salaries
- Taxation £5m
- Dividends £5m
- Profit reinvested into business £7m

What the value added pays for: Ted Baker

As the diagram above shows, value added is a necessity in business, not a luxury. Value added pays the wages, pays the bills and generates the profit needed to finance future growth. When starting up, every firm needs to think hard about whether the business idea adds enough value to be profitable. These are some business ideas that may have a market, yet do not have enough value added to be worthwhile:

- hand-washing cars
- a dog-walking service
- home-tutoring students on a one-to-one basis.

Good businesspeople recognise that high value added comes from clever ideas, presented well and delivered efficiently. That, in turn, makes it possible to run a sustainable, profitable business.

Revision essentials

Adding value: creating something of a higher value to a customer than its bought-in costs.
Unique selling point: a feature of a product or service that is not shared by any competitor.

Exercises

(A and B: 25 marks; 30 minutes)

A Read the unit, then ask yourself:

1. Why do staff rely on the business's skill at adding value? (2)
2. Briefly explain the sources of the added value in these cases:
   a) A £4 box of Celebrations chocolates. (3)
   b) A £48 ticket to see Chelsea play Newcastle. (3)
   c) A £2 cup of coffee at Starbucks. (3)
3. Identify the USP that each of these firms is keen to establish:
   a) Ryanair (1)
   b) L'Oréal. (1)
4. What might be the consequences of Ted Baker deciding to increase value added by cutting its £43 million spending on the clothes it buys in from suppliers? (4)

B The Oban Chocolate Company began in November 2003, backed by £9500 of funding from a local Scottish Islands enterprise agency. At their shop, cafe and factory premises in Oban, Helen Miller and Stewart MacKechnie make hand-made chocolates in the basement for sale upstairs. Good quality chocolate is not cheap, but by making fancy, unusual products, such as 'hot chilli truffles', value is added. Visitors also get a whole experience, including a visit downstairs to see the chocs being made. The problem, potentially, is that depending on tourists may mean very little trade in six to eight months of the year.

Unit 7 Understanding the need to add value

1 High value added is great for a business, but only if sales volumes are also high.

  a) Why may the Oban Chocolate Company have a problem? (4)

  b) What might they try to do to increase their sales volumes? (4)

Practice questions (20 marks; 25 minutes)

Callum and Jamie were bored with work. Both 21 years old, they had trained as plumbers, but it was getting dull working for British Gas. Jamie heard at a pub that there was a Snack Wagon for sale – fully equipped with gas, electricity and a fridge. Within three days they had found £3000 each to buy the van. Their plan was to place the van permanently on a busy road between Wimbledon and Croydon, then employ someone to do the cooking. Callum and Jamie's role would be to keep the van supplied and to make key decisions such as pricing.

The pricing decisions were largely drawn from their experience of local snack bars: teas and Cokes at around 60p, big burgers at about £1.50 and just the occasional item rising above £2. They were able to set down a few details, as shown in the table below.

In addition to these costs, there would be overhead costs such as rent, energy and labour costs. They allowed £350 per week for these. They served their first burgers in April and by October were making a modest profit. That same month they sold the business for £10,000. They had decided it was time to move out to Spain, to make a living from plumbing, and later to start up another business.

Pricing decisions for a Snack Wagon

Item	Components	Bought-in costs per unit	Selling price
Cup of tea	Bag, milk, sugar, plastic cup, spoon	8p	60p
Burger	Frozen hamburger, onions, bun, ketchup, paper napkins	25p	£1.50
Chips	Frozen chips, oil, paper cone, salt	15p	£1.00

Questions

1 How can a good location add value to a business such as Callum and Jamie's? (4)

2 a) How much value is added by making a cup of tea on this Snack Wagon? (2)

  b) Why would it be wrong to call this value added figure 'profit'? (4)

3 Outline two ways in which Callum and Jamie might have added more value to their snack bar, enabling the business to be more profitable. (4)

4 Discuss the limits to ever-greater added value, in a business such as this Snack Wagon. (6)

8 Invention and innovation

'Necessity, who is the mother of invention.'
Plato, The Republic, 44 BC

Invention means having a totally original idea, and showing how it can work in theory. **Innovation** means putting a new idea into practice. This could be either by bringing a new product to the market or by getting an organisation to try a new way of working.

Invention

In business, the ideal invention is one that can be patented. A **patent** makes it unlawful for anyone to copy your idea for 20 years after the patent has been taken out. This system provides the incentive for inventors. After all, if a bright new idea could be copied straight away, why spend time and effort in the first place? Many years without competition guarantees a high level of profit for the inventor.

The Patent Office will only grant a patent if the invention has never been shown publicly, if it is a significant step forward in thinking and if it has a practical application. A patent can be taken out on a new way of making something (e.g. the **Dyson** method for carpet sweeping, using 'cyclones' instead of vacuums).

Inventions have made huge differences to people's lives. They include the internal combustion engine (invented in the nineteenth century, and still the way petrol-driven cars work); the television; and many life-saving drugs such as penicillin (kills bacteria) or warfarin (stops blood clots). Not all inventions are so significant, yet small-scale changes can be important for businesses. The Walls ice cream **Solero** was launched in the early 1990s, backed by a patented method for creating a smooth-textured fruit ice. Before then, ice lollies always had a glass-like, hard texture. The effect was huge, with the Solero brand achieving sales in excess of £1000 million in Europe alone.

'An amazing invention – but who would ever want to use one?'
Rutherford Hayes, having made a call on Alexander Graham Bell's telephone in 1876 (Source: thinkexist.com)

For a new, small business, patenting an invention can be a difficult, expensive start. The problem is partly that the fees charged by the Patent Office may be quite high, possibly amounting to thousands of pounds. More serious still is that breaking a patent is not a criminal offence. So there are no police raids on those who unlawfully copy a patented idea. The patent holder has to take the copier to court – and that is expensive. Despite this, the huge success of James Dyson's patented 'dual cyclone' cleaners has shown the value of spending a bit of time and money on obtaining patents. The table below shows some examples of great inventions that were not patented, meaning the inventor received little or nothing.

Great inventions that were not patented

Invention	Invented by	Exploited by
The World Wide Web	Tim Berners-Lee, Britain	Yahoo, Google and many others
Light bulbs	Thomas Edison, America	Philips
Internal combustion engine	Nikolaus Otto, Germany	Daimler, then everyone else

Innovation

> 'Innovation distinguishes between a leader and a follower.'
> Steve Jobs, founder of Apple and the man behind the iPod (Source: Woopidoo.com)

The company that makes the best use of a new idea may not be its inventor. The innovator is the person or company that finds a way to make a new idea work. There are two types of innovation.

1. **Product innovation:** new product ideas brought to the marketplace, such as probiotic yogurt drinks (Actimel, Yakult, etc.).
2. **Process innovation:** new ways of working (e.g. McDonald's use of factory-style production in its restaurants; before McDonald's, food was made to order, which was slower and more expensive).

Some companies make innovation their key competitive advantage, such as **L'Oréal** in hair care or **Danone** in foods. Ten years ago, the best example would have been **Sony** in electronics, but the company has lost out in many sectors, such as televisions. As Sony's innovativeness declined, so did its sales and profits. By contrast, L'Oréal has become the world's biggest cosmetics business, largely through continuous innovation. Anyone wanting a hair colour product would trust that any L'Oréal product would be at the cutting edge.

In effect, gaining an image as an innovative company is a way of adding value. It makes your brands worth more to the consumer. Are you worth it? Of course you are.

Revision essentials
Innovation: putting a new idea into practice.
Invention: showing how an original idea can work in theory.
Patent: registering a new way of producing something, to establish sole rights to its use.

Exercises

(20 marks; 25 minutes)

Read the unit, then ask yourself:

1. Give two reasons why a successful patent is likely to lead to high profits for the inventor. (2)
2. Reread the section about patents under the heading 'Invention' (page 29) and then explain why a brand name cannot be patented. (4)
3. Are the following examples of product innovation or process innovation?
    a) a new car fuelled by solar power (launched in Spain, not Britain) (1)
    b) a cinema chain changing from a national call centre to providing the telephone number of the local cinema (1)
    c) a new service offering door-to-door collection and delivery of dry cleaning. (1)
4. Innovation can be expensive, for example L'Oréal's stream of new product launches. Why is it vital, therefore, that innovative products should have high added value? (4)
5. Reread Steve Jobs' quote about innovation (page 30).
    a) Explain what it means. (3)
    b) Explain why it matters in business to be a leader rather than a follower. (4)

Practice questions

(20 marks; 25 minutes)

Innovation in car sales

August 2005 was a poor month for car sales in America. Sales fell, especially for bigger trucks and 4×4 vehicles. A rare bright spot was the 115 per cent increase in the sales of the Toyota Prius. This innovative car offers a combined petrol and electric engine. In town it runs in electric silence, with no exhaust emissions and with terrific fuel economy. If the driver wants to put his/her foot down, the on-board computer kicks in the petrol engine, so that the car can overtake or reach a 70 mph motorway cruising speed.

First launched in 1997, the Prius was seen as an oddity by the motor industry. With, in effect, two engines, it cost about £3000 more to make a Prius. Yet Toyota only charged an extra £2000 for it. Sales were poor and profits much poorer. Then in 2003 Hollywood stars took up the car, to show off their environmental consciences. Even more importantly, the leap in petrol prices in 2004 and 2005 made it seem a sensible choice for ordinary drivers. Demand blossomed, leading to a three-month waiting list for the cars in August and September 2005. Toyota's innovation started to pay off.

SECTION 1 Spotting a business opportunity

Questions

1 a) If 8000 Prius cars were sold in America in August 2004, how many were sold in 2005? (3)

  b) Explain what could cause a three-month waiting list for those wishing to buy the Prius. (4)

2 During 2005 many American and European car producers announced that they were starting work on their own hybrid cars.

  a) Outline two reasons why they waited so long after Toyota's 1997 launch of the Prius. (4)

  b) Discuss whether the other American and European companies may have left it too late to succeed by copying Toyota's approach. (6)

3 How might the image of all Toyota's car models be affected by its success with the Prius? (3)

9 Assessing a franchise opportunity

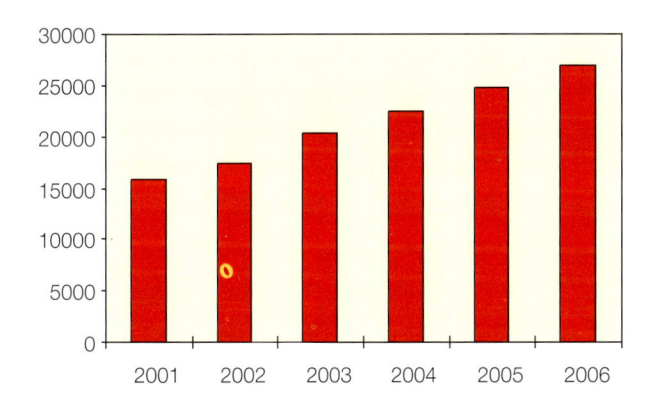

Number of Subway sandwich outlets worldwide

When you have set up a business successfully in one location, the race is on to do the same elsewhere. If you do not 'copy' your idea, others will. Yet how can a small business quickly clone its own idea, many times over? It is hard to start up one business outlet, let alone lots of them.

One answer to this problem is franchising. This means selling the rights to use your business idea and methods at a specific location or area. The person or business buying the rights therefore has to do all the work to make it a success. You, as the franchise owner, must ensure you select someone who will do a good job – and therefore not damage the image of your business.

Currently, there is no better example of this than the **Subway** chain of sandwich shops. It was started in 1965 by a 17-year-old (Fred de Luca) in America. He borrowed $1000 and set up a single outlet. Its success led him to open others, but he saw much bigger prospects, so started selling franchises in 1974. By 2005 there were 24,750 Subway outlets worldwide, boasting sales of more than £6000 million a year. The first Subway came to Britain in 1996 and there are nearly 200 today. By 2010 the company hopes for 2000 franchise outlets in Britain – the same number as **McDonald's**. Subway's success has forced McDonald's and **Burger King** to start selling their own versions of 'deli' sandwiches.

What's in it for the franchise owner?

Expanding a business is expensive and difficult. Opening stores requires a huge amount of capital. For example, a Burger King typically costs £500,000. Selling franchises brings money in, instead of paying it out;

and it saves having to employ huge numbers of managers to check up on every aspect of the store openings. Key benefits of expanding by selling franchises include:

- Enables a firm to expand its sales quickly; this helps fill gaps that other firms will fill if you do not get there first.
- Franchise owners not only sell a franchise, but also receive a share of all future sales. Burger King (the franchise owner) receives 5 per cent of the sales revenue of every one of the 11,000 outlets worldwide; in addition, every outlet has to buy their supplies from Burger King, so the central company makes profits there too.
- You, the franchise owner, can concentrate on developing new products and services, and on good marketing and advertising; this was the basis of McDonald's huge success for many years.

Why buy a franchise rather than start up independently?

Starting a business from scratch requires a remarkable range of skills. Anyone can have a bright idea; and lots of people are good at one thing – cooking, perhaps. Yet there is a huge gap between being a good cook and running a successful restaurant. More than anything else you need to:

- identify a menu and an image that customers want
- work out how to run the operation efficiently
- find the right suppliers
- market your business effectively.

It is not surprising that half of all new restaurants close within three years.

Key benefits of buying a franchise include:

- Not only buying your part of an image (e.g. McDonald's or BSM – the British School of Motoring), but also a method for doing things (e.g. the equipment for making a milkshake, plus the instructions on how to make it, clean the equipment, and so on).
- An individual outlet could never afford image-building TV advertising; being part of Subway or McDonald's enables you to benefit from major marketing campaigns.
- The products and methods of working have been pre-tested, so the chance of mistakes is lower, therefore the failure rate is lower with franchise start-ups. This, in turn, means that banks are much more willing to lend to a franchise start-up than a brand new, independent operation.

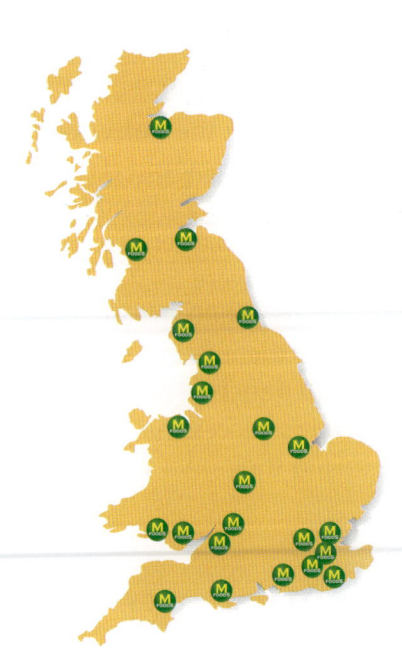

A franchise start-up takes on the brand, products and methods used by the other outlets

Why might an entrepreneur not want to buy a franchise?

Franchising is a halfway house towards running your own independent business. As a **franchisee** you are bound by the rules of the franchise owner. This might be very frustrating for an experienced businessperson who wants to be their own boss. The rules may force them to offer products that might sell well nationally, but not locally. Among the other possible drawbacks are that:

- **royalty** payments of as much as 8 per cent of revenue are common. A typical franchise outlet might have an annual sales figure of about £300,000, so an annual payment of £24,000 is being made. That is no problem when things are going well, but between 2002 and 2005 sales at UK McDonald's outlets fell by 25 per cent. It would be very annoying to pay large royalties when sales and profits are falling
- not all franchises are good ones. The Pierre Victoire chain of restaurants had over 100 franchise outlets when it collapsed; franchisees were left with no back-up and a terrible image from a failed business.

Conclusion

'There are a lot of cowboys around.'
Sir Bernard Ingham, president of the British Franchise Association

As with any other business opportunity, buying a franchise carries major risks. The buyer needs to check the financial records of the franchise owner and talk to existing franchisees to find out whether they are happy with the service they are getting for their royalty payments. Without doubt, though, buying a good franchise is one of the best ways to start your own business. Having had success with a franchise, an **entrepreneur** could try to start up something completely new later on.

Revision essentials
Entrepreneur: someone who takes on the risk of starting up a new enterprise.
Franchisee: someone who buys and runs a franchise outlet.
Royalties: paying a percentage of the sales revenue generated by a business or product.

Exercises

(A and B: 25 marks; 30 minutes)

A Read the unit, then ask yourself:

1 Give two reasons why it is hard to develop a business rapidly. (2)
2 Identify two qualities Fred de Luca must have had to start his own business at the age of 17. (2)
3 Outline two problems that might arise if the franchise owner sold franchises to businesspeople who cut corners to make high profits without high standards. (4)
4 Why would a bank be more willing to lend money to someone opening a franchise outlet than someone opening a fully independent business? (5)

B Ian Janes had spent 10 frustrating years as a journalist, working on a shipping magazine. He had been saving for several years to start his own business. He had £45,000 in the bank and a burning desire to prove to his wife and parents that he could be a financial success. Ian loved eating out, and wanted to start a bar/restaurant. Now he had to decide whether or not to buy into a franchise operation such as Pizza Hut, or start something completely independently. He knew that, if necessary, he could borrow up to £100,000 on the value of the house he owned jointly with his wife.

1 Outline two reasons for and two reasons against Ian deciding to buy a franchise. (4)
2 Recommend whether he should buy a franchise or go independent. Explain your answer. (8)

Practice questions

(20 marks; 25 minutes)

With Burger King, McDonald's and Pizza Hut all struggling in recent years, the most attractive-looking franchise opportunity is probably Subway. To start up, you have to pay a £6000 fee, and then gain approval from the company. They will check your financial position, your business experience and your hunger for success. If accepted, you will need to pay about £100,000 to get a store decorated and equipped by Subway's suppliers.

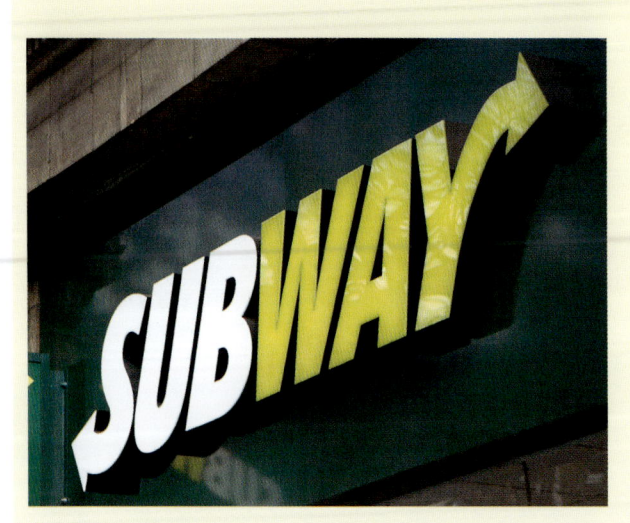

Once opened, you pay Subway 8 per cent of sales revenue as a fee, plus 3.5 per cent into the national fund for advertising. You will have the franchise for 20 years, with an option on another 20 years. With the average Subway outlet having sales of £250,000 a year, it is quite hard to see it as a hugely profitable business. Yet 70 per cent of franchisees go on to buy a second franchise, so they must be doing very well. An impressive feature of the Subway model is its flexibility. Although most customers buy huge, foot-long, calorie-filled sandwiches, Subway has introduced a '7 under 6' promotion of 7 sandwiches that have fewer than 6 g of fat. This is part of a deliberate marketing strategy to avoid McDonald's problem of being associated with obesity.

Questions

1. Explain why someone wanting to start a business might wish to become a Subway franchisee. (3)
2. Outline three benefits the Subway company receives from selling additional franchises. (6)
3. **a)** How much is a franchisee with the average level of sales having to pay Subway each year? (3)
   b) Identify two benefits the franchisee is receiving for the money they are paying each year. (2)
4. Unlike Subway, some franchise owners take the franchisee's money and give very little in return. Explain two ways in which a businessperson should check out a franchise owner before handing over their money. (6)

SECTION 2

SHOWING ENTERPRISE

10 Introduction to enterprise skills

In August 2004 Duncan Goose gave up his day job to start a new type of business. He wanted to sell bottled water at a profit, but use all the profits for charity. The charity was to be Roundabout, which helps tackle one of the biggest problems for African villagers – water. Villagers may have to walk a mile to a well, then pump the water by hand, then walk home with a full container. Roundabout puts a kids' roundabout on the well-head, so that when the children play, water is pumped up into a water tank above ground. Now villagers can get their water by turning a tap. Duncan's water is called **One**. Do look out for it.

To make One work required a huge range of enterprise skills. Duncan had to:

- **ask why?** Why did consumers put up with overpriced bottled water – often priced higher than milk, orange juice or Coke?
- **ask why not?** Why not have a not-for-profit water that could make people feel happy to pay the price?
- **think creatively** – about what to do with the profits; choosing a water charity makes the One story complete
- **do it!** Many people talk about great ideas, but Duncan actually got up and did it. He spent months finding a suitable supplier of water, reading the laws that govern the sale of water and setting up the One website (www.we-are-one.org.uk)
- **show initiative.** When Bob Geldof announced the Live8 concerts in May 2005, Duncan found a way to make contact. One was approved as the only water available backstage at Live8 – gaining millions of pounds' worth of publicity.

Just do it

> *'Anyone who has never made a mistake has never tried anything new.'*
> Albert Einstein

In 1988 **Nike** launched the advertising tag line 'Just do it'. It helped the business grow to the multibillion dollar empire it is today. The phrase sums up the key enterprise skill, which is to make things happen.

Most adults watch too much and do too little. They watch football instead of play it. They watch soaps instead of talking to each other. They watch programmes about people building their own houses, but stay in their armchairs.

Being enterprising means spotting an opportunity, then having a go. Of course, this could be disastrous. A family may be rescued from a mountainside, having gone climbing without proper equipment or training. In this case, 'let's just do it' is reckless. Similarly, businesses are set up by people who have no expertise, no skills and not enough capital. Yet a few examples of stupidity should not put people off. Bold ideas lead to exciting lives and potentially huge rewards – emotionally and financially.

Taking calculated risks

> *'Great successes never come without risks.'*
> Flavius Josephus (around AD 65)

Risk is about chance. What is the chance that a particular outcome will occur? Large firms know that, over the years, only one in five new products is a success. So the chance of failure is four out of five. Does that mean firms should never launch new products? No, or eventually they will go out of business. They must either:

- make enough profit from existing products to fund five new product launches for every one success; or
- make sure that the one success is big enough to make up for the failures.

> *'Educated risks are the key to success.'*
> William Olsen, chief executive

In 2004 the giant company Reckitt Benckiser analysed the £550 million UK market for household cleaning products. It appeared saturated with brands such as Cif, Mr Muscle, Dettol and Harpic. But Reckitt believed there was room for a product that would be seen as 'the *most* powerful cleaner'. It launched **Cillit Bang** with a brilliant, eye-catching TV commercial. The risk was great, but it has been a huge success. Sales have risen sharply within the Reckitt division that produces Cillit Bang.

What was the risk of failure? The development and launch costs of a product such as this are about £15 million. What was the benefit from success? A sales potential of between £50 and £100 million a year, generating profits of perhaps £20 to £50 million a year. That was a risk worth taking.

SECTION 2 Showing enterprise

Becoming enterprising: what they did and how they did it

Who?	What?	How?
Richard Branson, Virgin	At 16, Branson left school to start a student magazine. His Virgin Group is now worth many £ billions. Key qualities: initiative; risk taking; a talent for publicity.	Branson has shown an unusual ability to spot opportunities, build a positive image for a business, then sell it on at a profit. He has had many flops (Virgin Cola, Virgin Bride, etc.), but the successes far outweigh the flops.
Bill Gates, Microsoft	Bill Gates founded Microsoft, aged 19, and today is the wealthiest man in the world. Key qualities: technical brilliance; determined; ruthless.	Together with Paul Allen, Gates wrote some brilliant software that was adopted by IBM in the earliest personal computers. Gates was quick to spot the business potential of software and the need to dominate a market.
Sergey Brin and Larry Page, Google	In their mid-20s, they borrowed money to start Google in 1998; by 2005 it was valued at over $75 billion. Key qualities: brilliant; creative.	Brin and Page not only had the genius to invent the Google search engine, but also persuaded a Californian investor to write out a cheque for $100,000 to 'Google, Inc.' before they had even opened a bank account.
Perween Warsi, S&A Foods	Warsi began cooking Indian food in her kitchen, for sale locally, and built ready-meal specialist S&A Foods to a turnover of nearly £100m. Key qualities: passionate; determined; a risk taker.	Warsi started by employing five women to work in her family kitchen; she pestered Asda for six months before they tried her products, then rented a factory when Asda gave her a contract. S&A Foods now produces Thai, Indian and Italian meals for Tesco and Asda. Warsi is one of Britain's richest women.

Exercises

(A and B: 25 marks; 30 minutes)

A Read the unit, then ask yourself:

1 Why could 'just having a go' be disastrous? (3)
2 Does being enterprising have to be about making money? (3)
3 What is the evidence that launching Cillit Bang was a risk worth taking? (4)
4 Outline one example of enterprise you have seen recently. It could be in your local high street or in a non-business setting. (5)

B On the first day of the 2005/6 Premiership season, Fulham introduced a new idea. By the manager's dugout were two exercise bikes for substitutes to warm up. Manager Chris Coleman said the idea was to bring the heart rate of the subs up to the level of the players on the pitch. This could help reduce warm-up injuries.

1 What 'Why?' question had the Fulham staff been asking themselves? (2)
2 Was the Fulham management being enterprising? Explain your answer. (5)
3 How might the players feel about this new idea? (3)

Practice questions

(20 marks; 30 minutes)

SCHOOLBOY LAUNCHES AIRLINE

BY CORINNE ABRAMS

The Sun, 19 July 2005

A SCHOOLBOY took his A level business studies coursework one step further than his fellow pupils – by launching his own airline. Enterprising Daniel Reilly was inspired to set up his Nexus Airlines after completing his project on low-cost airlines. The 18-year-old, from Maghull, Merseyside, is thought to be the youngest chief executive of an airline in the world. He is leasing a Boeing 737 plane from an airline based in Palma.

'I've always been interested in aviation so I decided to do my A level business studies project on setting up an airline. I called round a few airlines and asked how they had done it and I slowly realised it was quite achievable.'

Daniel, who attends Deyes High School in Maghull, showed his project to a financial adviser who found backers for the business. Initially the airline will operate services from Liverpool John Lennon Airport to Tenerife, Gran Canaria, Lanzarote and Fuerteventura from its new headquarters in Bradford, West Yorkshire.

Customers will be able to book flights – which cost from £50 one-way – from Friday, with the first flights taking off on November 1 this year. He said: 'Most of my school friends are now going off to university but I'm in charge of an airline. I don't know if I will be the next Richard Branson but I certainly wouldn't say no.'

Questions

1 **a)** Identify two enterprising qualities shown by Daniel. (2)
   b) Explain which of the two you thought the more important, and why. (6)
2 If the Liverpool–Canary Islands flights are successful, bigger rivals such as easyJet and Ryanair might copy Nexus Airways. How should Daniel plan to cope with a competitor? (6)
3 Go to Daniel's website (www.nexusairways.com) and look up the latest news of his business. Outline how well the business seems to be doing. (6)

11 Thinking creatively

Why?

> 'Disneyland will never be completed, as long as there is imagination left in the world.'
> Walt Disney (1901–66)

Creative thinking stems from asking questions. Three-year-olds can drive their parents crazy by constantly asking why. 'Why are those sweets in the toilet?' (A condom machine) 'Why are raspberries red?' and so on. In fact, just such a question about raspberries made the producer of **Slush Puppy** decide to make the raspberry flavour a blue colour. Then the red and blue would make a more eye-catching display.

When kids start going to school, they soon learn that asking why is not welcome. Teachers want to get on with things, not get bogged down in lots of questions. More is the pity. The ability to ask why is at the root of creativity and innovation.

Some significant 'Why?' questions of recent times are set out in the table below.

Significant 'Why?' questions

The 'Why?' question	The answer	The business response
Why are oil supplies running down?	Rising car ownership worldwide.	Hybrid cars, part petrol and part battery, such as the fuel-efficient Toyota Prius.
Why are people getting fatter?	Too much fatty fast food.	McDonald's menu changes towards salads, vegetables and fruit.
Why do older women look older?	Wrinkles and loose skin.	Anti-ageing, antiwrinkle and firming creams.

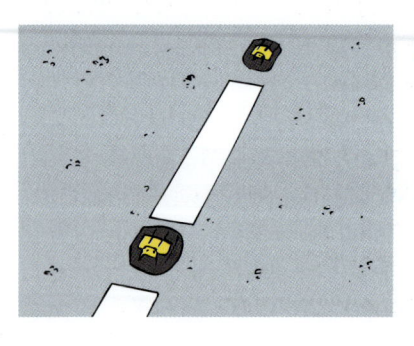

Why not?

It is also vital to ask 'Why not?' The three-year-old is trying to find out the way the world is. Creative thinkers also ask why the world cannot be different. In 1933 Percy Shaw became the inventor of one of the world's most widely used ideas. Driving home in dense fog he nearly drove off the road and crashed, but was saved by the flashing eye of a cat sitting on a fence.

Two years later he patented 'Catseyes', the invention that made him a fortune. Brilliantly, he made a reflector with a rubberised top that would give when cars ran over it. And the action of pushing down the rubber top wipes the reflector clean – just like a cat's eye blinking.

Many 'Why not?' questions are much less significant than Percy Shaw's; for example, Why not have a strawberry-flavour Calippo ice lolly? It is an obvious idea, but might prove significant if the new product is a huge success.

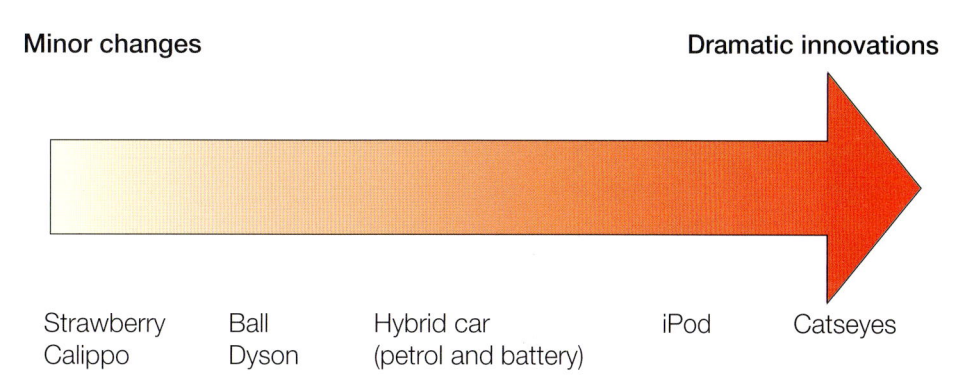

Minor changes → Dramatic innovations

Creativity scale: Strawberry Calippo | Ball Dyson | Hybrid car (petrol and battery) | iPod | Catseyes

Managing creativity

Most of us have lots of creative thoughts. We look in an ice cream cabinet and wish for a mint choc ice or a mango lolly. The problem is that we may not tell anybody about these thoughts, or – worse – we may try to tell someone, but find that nobody listens. It follows that creativity may only have meaning if it is backed up by effective communication. Percy Shaw had his idea and developed it himself. Most of us have neither the money nor the ability to achieve this.

Well-run businesses encourage the sharing of creative thoughts. Great ideas may come from the shop floor as much as from management. Good managers encourage this. The ghastly superbug MRSA arises from poor hygiene in hospitals. Good, well-motivated staff should quickly come up with ideas on how to stop it. Unfortunately, many NHS managers think they know best, so the problem remains acute.

For some businesses, creativity is the basis of the operation. A good example is **Codemasters Ltd**, a UK private company that produces games software. It has grown from a bedroom in 1986 to employing 450 people on a 90-acre site in Warwickshire. It is

'An essential aspect of creativity is not being afraid to fail.'
Edwin Land, inventor of the Polaroid camera

Sharing creative thoughts with colleagues is good for business

Unit 11 Thinking creatively

45

> 'The man who has no imagination has no wings.'
> Muhammad Ali, greatest ever boxer

Europe's largest privately owned software business. Among its key games are Brian Lara Cricket, Colin McRae Rally and LMA Football Manager. A quick visit to its website (www.codemasters.co.uk) shows the importance of creativity. It also shows the potential rewards, as 44 jobs were being advertised in August 2005, including software development jobs at up to £60,000 plus bonuses.

Exercises

(20 marks; 20 minutes)

Read the unit, then ask yourself:

1 Outline two benefits from asking the question 'Why?' (4)
2 What might be the answer and the business response (see table on page 44) to the following questions?
   a) Why are organic foods so expensive? (4)
   b) Why has Sainsbury's lost out so badly to Tesco? (4)
3 Suggest two ways in which managers can encourage staff to be creative. (2)
4 Why is creativity particularly important for staff in a business such as Codemasters? (6)

Classroom exercise

(This should take about 20 minutes; if longer, ask each group leader to give some feedback; someone could summarise each group's answers on a whiteboard or flip chart.) Get into groups of about four people and appoint a leader. The leader's job is to appoint a secretary/note-taker, and to make sure everyone answers the following questions:

1 Which are your top three favourite chocolate 'countlines' (bars, bags or tubes of sweets you pick off the shop counter)?
2 Describe how you eat your favourite chocolate countline (probe: 'in detail, please').
3 Are there any bars you dislike? Why?
4 How many countlines have you eaten in the past seven days?
5 What is your opinion of these three ideas for new countlines?
   a) CrunchieFlake: a chocolate flake studded with pieces of Crunchie honeycomb.
   b) FizzyFruits: chocolate-coated balls containing fizzy fruit candy in different flavours.
   c) Crisp 'n' Cool: a Cadbury milk chocolate bar wrapped in special foil that keeps it from melting.

Probe – for each idea, find out:
- Whether the group would buy it to try it.
- What price they think it would be.
- Whether they think they would buy it regularly.
- Which of the three they think would be the biggest seller and why?

6 Ask everyone to stop for a moment to consider whether they can think of a great new countline. Get them to be as detailed as possible; get the comments of others.

12 Deliberate creativity

Most people think that great ideas come from flashes of inspiration. There is the famous story of Isaac Newton in his garden, seeing an apple fall to the ground and thinking 'gravity'. In fact, most creative ideas can be put down to patterns of thought. They have specific causes that lead logically to answers.

Take the **Apple iPod**, which fused the idea of portable music (from the Sony Walkman), MP3 downloading, portable hard-drive storage (from laptops) and smart design (from Apple computers). Nothing revolutionary, but the parts were combined together to generate a brilliant multibillion pound innovation.

Professor Dennis Sherwood has been studying creativity for many years. He believes people can be taught to come up with bright new ideas. He calls this method **deliberate creativity**.

The essence of deliberate creativity is to get groups of people focused on what they know; to describe, perhaps, the TV show *Who Wants to be a Millionaire?* If 6 people each write down 10 things about *Millionaire*, some will be duplicated, but many points will be different. Perhaps 30–40 different points will emerge. These might range from 'a £1 million top prize' to 'one player sits in the centre, facing the questioner, in the middle of the audience'.

Having described the topic in detail, the trick is to focus on one element and ask how it might be different. What if the player didn't 'sit in the centre, facing the questioner, in the middle of the audience'? How else might things be done?

Perhaps a quiz show might be less relaxed and more edgy if the player and the questioner were standing up? And what if there were no audience? And perhaps more than one player? This way of thinking enabled the BBC to devise *The Weakest Link* soon after *Millionaire* became a TV sensation. Later, the presenter role was developed further in the worldwide TV success *Deal or No Deal*.

> 'The secret to creativity is knowing how to hide your sources.'
> Albert Einstein, genius

The professor's key point is that ordinary people can come up with good new ideas if they are helped to think through a deliberate process. In his book *Innovation and Creativity*, Professor Sherwood recalls a workshop he held with managers at Nestlé, the maker of KitKat and Yorkie. When someone wrote down about chocolate that 'you eat it', he asked the questions: How might this be different? What else might we do with chocolate? Among the answers came:

- Use it as a fragrance, for perfumed soaps, shampoos, air fresheners, and so on.
- As a fire alarm(!) – using its melting point as a way of identifying that a room was getting dangerously hot.

These unusual ideas came from people who would never think of themselves as 'creative'.

Evaluating ideas

Coming up with great ideas is not enough, however. There remain two key stages:

1. Evaluating whether a 'great idea' is also a good, sensible, workable idea.
2. Bringing the idea to reality.

> 'By far the greatest flow of newness is not innovation at all. It is imitation.'
> Theodore Levitt, management guru

To judge a new idea, Professor Sherwood recommends the clever approach of another professor – Edward de Bono (mainly famous for mind maps). De Bono warns that people in groups influence each other. A good new idea might be rejected because one individual is in a bad mood. He therefore suggests that those involved in evaluating ideas should have specific, different roles (one cheerleader, one cautious, etc.). Professor Sherwood uses this approach to suggest that there are seven key roles, often represented as different coloured hats (i.e. whoever wears the hat has to fulfil that role). These seven key roles (or hats) are as follows:

- **Benefits (yellow hat):** identifying the number and likely scale of the benefits.
- **Issues to be managed (black hat):** identifying the risks and how they are to be managed.
- **Constituencies and feelings (red hat):** which groups of people will be affected by the idea, what is their likely reaction and how can these factors be managed?
- **Data (white hat):** what data do we have and do we still need to take an informed decision? How reliable are the sources? And how do we handle uncertainty in the data?
- **Solutions (green hat):** what solutions can we identify to the problems identified by the black, red and white hats? How can they be overcome?
- **Actions (purple hat):** what actions should we take? Have we enough information to take a decision now? Or should we carry on with the analysis phase?

'The creativity that emerges from the company comes from the many ideas of the people who are here.'
John Rollwagen, chief executive

Process (blue hat): who will be responsible for what, if we carry the project forward?

(Source: Sherwood, D., 2001, *Smart Things to Know About Innovation and Creativity*, Capstone)

The point is simple. Staff will only generate ideas if they feel they are given a fair hearing. If bright ideas are encouraged, but then quietly killed off in the evaluation phase, no one will waste time coming up with more. The coloured hats approach ensures that every idea is given a chance.

Of course, good ideas can still fail if they are poorly carried out. The cost overruns on the Channel Tunnel have condemned the project to being permanently unprofitable. It simply cost too much to build. And many newly launched soft drinks or chocolate bars sound great, but simply do not taste quite right. Those practical problems can be put down to poor management.

Exercises

(A and B: 25 marks; 30 minutes)

A Read the unit, then ask yourself:

1 What evidence is given that the iPod may have been a result of deliberate creativity rather than inspiration? (3)
2 Use the chapter to identify four steps to achieving successful deliberate creativity. (4)
3 Why might it be useful to give the yellow hat to the person who has come up with the idea being discussed? (3)
4 How might a firm such as Tesco encourage staff to come up with new ideas for improving the business? (5)

B Encouraging and using ideas 'from the floor' can have dramatic results, as at BMW Group Plant Oxford. In February 2004 the BMW Group announced that suggestions from staff at Oxford had saved the company £10.5 million in two years. Of the 14,333 suggestions staff had put forward, three-quarters were put into action. They ranged from cutting unnecessary use of paper to more complex engineering solutions.

1 Give two possible reasons for turning down a number of the suggestions. (2)
2 What is the most likely explanation for the high number of suggestions from the Oxford staff? Explain your reasoning. (3)
3 Discuss whether the staff should get a financial reward for the suggestions that are put into action. (5)

Unit 12 Deliberate creativity

Practice questions

(20 marks; 25 minutes)

Ideas are the new currency

Businesses and organisations want creativity from their employees and see it as a key competitive advantage in a modern economy.

A small printing business in Northampton was suffering from increased competition. It was having to cut its prices by 5 per cent every year. It was clear that the business needed to do things in a better way. After a Friday night 'meeting' at a bar, the boss and five staff members agreed that changes were needed. The following week, two of the staff took a day off to attend a course on web design. They had spotted that people who needed printing done locally were also short of the expertise to design websites. Within three months the company had signed seven of its customers up for websites at an average price of £800.

This was a creative solution to a problem. But can we all be creative? The business thinker Edward de Bono believes that: 'As with any skill (cooking or skiing for instance) some people will become more skilful than others. But everyone can learn to be creative. It is not a mystical gift.'

Questions

1 a) Outline two ways companies could benefit from a more creative workforce. (4)

  b) Explain how a company's sales revenues might be affected by doing things 'in a better way'. (5)

2 Dr de Bono says 'everyone can learn to be creative'. Explain how this view compares with the ideas of Professor Dennis Sherwood. (5)

3 Do you think that we can all be creative? Explain your thoughts on this topic. (6)

13 Business risks and rewards

In 2004 Trevor Peake put all his savings – £22,000 – into opening a clothes shop. He had always loved black, gothic clothes, and thought that a specialist shop could succeed in South London. Short of capital from the start, Trevor never had the range of stock he wanted. He also had neither the money for advertising nor the time to wait until word spread that this was the place for goths to come. Four months after it opened, his shop closed down. After he sold off his stock (very cheaply) and paid his debts, Trevor was left with just over £400.

Business is risky – at every stage and at all times. Even giants such as **McDonald's**, **Coca-Cola** and **Marks and Spencer** have suffered just when most people thought they were too big to suffer. The riskiest stage of all, though, is at the beginning. Of new businesses 36 per cent fold within three years, and only 10 per cent make significant profits.

Risks can yield rewards

In 1984 two teenagers, Richard and David Darling, moved on from playing computer games to writing them. They produced the games for fun, but then tried advertising them in a popular computer weekly. A £70 advertisement brought in £7000 worth of orders. In 1986 they formed a company, **Codemasters Ltd**. It went on to produce some of the longest-lasting games software brands, such as Colin McRae Rally and LMA Football Manager. In summer 2005 it held the number one spot in the games chart with Brian Lara Cricket. Today the business has over £100 million of sales per year, employs over 400 people and is worth around £250 million. Risking £70 on an advertisement has resulted in fabulous wealth and an amazing achievement.

What are the main risks?

> *'You miss 100 percent of the shots you never take.'*
> Wayne Gretsky, US ice hockey star

Businesses start when one or two people have an idea and push it through. It may be a market stall; it may be a shop; or it may be a scientific or design breakthrough. Putting it into practice will be difficult, because there are so many things to think about and so many things to get right. At the start, the main pitfalls are:

1. **Making sure you really know what the customer wants.** If a new business is to succeed, it must have something new and different. It cannot just be one more pizza takeaway. Whatever is unique about the new business is a risk. Customers must be attracted to the unique feature, and stay attracted. In the 1990s Cadbury launched a series of new chocolate products (Strollers, Wispa, Wispa Gold). All sold well for a while, as people bought one or two. But over time they drifted back to their regular favourites, and these brands have been dropped.

2. **Making sure you can deliver on your promises.** Many new firms generate hype, but let the customers down (e.g. the 'great new club' that proves a bit dull, or the clothes shop that never seems to stock your size or the colour you want).

3. **Getting the financing right.** The single most common reason for start-up failure is lack of working capital. Entrepreneurs work out how much will be needed for the builders, the equipment, the computers and the vehicles. Yet they underestimate the need for capital to keep the business going day by day – to pay the wages, the suppliers, the gas bills, and so on. This daily (working) capital will eventually be funded by the revenue coming in from customers, but many firms start slowly. A shop in Leeds that sells sports trophies took three years before the revenues were sufficient to support the business. (Now it is thriving, but the owner is thankful that he was able to borrow £16,000 from his mother to tide him over this difficult period.)

What are the main risks?

At the start	In the early days	When growth is rapid
Identifying a market gap big enough to be profitable.	Making sure your initial customers come back for more.	'Overtrading' – sales growing faster than you can cope with financially.
Raising (more than) enough capital.	Running out of cash during the off-season.	Struggling to manage rapid rises in staff, especially middle management.
Getting the right people working in the right way.	Running out of energy and self-belief when times are tough.	The entrepreneur owner may struggle to be a good manager.
Building a base of initial customers.	Coping with competition when it arrives.	The boss and staff may become complacent, so the rise leads to the fall.

What are the main rewards?

Becoming wealthy

Starting a small business can generate huge returns. Most working people struggle to save much from their salary. They may be comfortable, but can never become rich. Starting a business creates the possibility of selling it once it is established. It could be sold completely, or part of it could be sold to outside shareholders, by 'floating' the business on the stock market. In 1990 Tim Slade and Jules Leaver raised £12,000 to open their first **Fat Face** sportswear shop. In May 2005 they sold the business for £100 million. They had planned to float Fat Face on the stock market, but a private buyer offered a better deal.

In 1972 a 23-year-old started a market stall in London, selling clothes imported from Thailand. A year later he used the profits from the stall to open his first shop, calling it **Monsoon**. The business kept growing, largely from reinvested profits, and Peter Simon (the founder) kept adding new stores. In 1984 he spotted the opportunity for a new type of shop, **Accessorize**. Today there are over 250 Monsoon and Accessorize shops and the business makes annual profits of around £50 million. The Simon family still owns 75 per cent of the business, making them one of the richest families in Britain.

The excitement

Excitement comes from taking risks (i.e. the risks generate the rewards). It is the difference between riding a bike on the flat and riding it down a steep hill; or watching Brazil play football compared with watching Germany. At every stage in starting and building a business, risks have to be taken and new skills have to be learnt. This provides the buzz that makes it exciting to be an entrepreneur.

The control

Many people dislike being told what to do, especially if they do not respect their boss. For such people, starting up on their own may be ideal. They can then make their own decisions and, if necessary, their own compromises. People with this motivation may struggle, though, if they start to employ others who have different ideas or standards from their own.

> *'I've been rich and I've been poor. Rich is better.'*
> Frank Sinatra, singer and actor

> *'The man who makes no mistake does not usually make anything.'*
> William Magee, philosopher, 1889

> *'Rewards should be proportionate to risk.'*
> Harvard Business Review, 1986

Exercises

(A and B: 20 marks; 30 minutes)

A Read the unit, then ask yourself:

1. What did Trevor Peake do wrong? (3)
2. If you are opening your own shop, how can you make sure that you really know what the customer wants? (3)
3. How does the experience of Peter Simon compare with the three points made under the heading 'What are the main rewards?'? (4)
4. Of new businesses 36 per cent close within three years. Should that put people off starting up on their own? (5)

B On 26 July 2005 the low-cost airline EUJet collapsed, leaving passengers stranded. Chief executive P. J. McGoldrick had started the business in Ireland, then expanded to run routes from Kent. In June, half the aircrafts' seats flew empty, creating big operating losses. The business folded after the Bank of Scotland refused to lend any more money. The bank was already owed £22 million, secured against the company's assets.

1 Identify two problems EUJet may have faced at a time of rapid expansion. (2)

2 Is it fair that customers should share in the business risks faced by a newly started company? (3)

Practice questions (20 marks; 25 minutes)

Red Bull risks and (huge) rewards

In 1982 a jet-lagged 25-year-old Austrian (Dietrich Mateschitz) tried a cheap local energy drink while working in Thailand: 'It cured my jet lag in seconds'. The drink was called Krating Daeng, which translates as Red Bull. There had never been a product like it before in the West, either in taste or effect. It was packed with sugar, caffeine and taurine. Mateschitz spent years talking to the cautious Thai producer and in 1985 founded Red Bull GmbH in Austria. The Thai company received 51 per cent of the shares; Mateschitz had the other 49 per cent and was to be the chief executive (and still is).

Early taste tests were discouraging. 'Most people said it was disgusting and created a sticky mouth,' one former employee recalls. Bars initially refused to stock it, seeing it as an overpriced medicinal or health-related product, rather than a mixer. Mateschitz remained certain that it would be a hit. To create a youth-oriented 'underground' feel for Red Bull, he deliberately restricted supply and refused to advertise. He paid students and DJs to host parties where the drink was served. Young Austrians caught the bug and by the early 1990s Red Bull spread to Germany.

Red Bull was launched in Britain in 1993 and now sells over £100 million of high-priced cans in shops alone. Worldwide, Red Bull reached sales of $1 billion in 2001, and $2 billion by 2004. Also in 2004 Mateschitz decided to buy the Jaguar Formula 1 motor racing team for £60 million. This built on several years of sponsoring extreme sports – to back the Red Bull image as an edgy, though non-alcoholic, drink.

Mateschitz took huge risks, but has reaped huge rewards. The Red Bull business is believed to be worth well over £1000 million. It rivals Pepsi-Cola for profitability and worldwide impact. Quite an achievement for a cheap energy drink from Thailand.

Questions

1 a) Outline two risks Mateschitz faced when launching Red Bull in Europe. (4)
  b) Explain how he overcame these risks. (4)
2 Surprisingly, Red Bull has never faced competition from a major soft drinks firm. How well do you think a 'Coca-Cola Energy' drink might do today against Red Bull? (6)
3 Discuss what Mateschitz has gained from starting up Red Bull, using the three factors identified under the heading, 'What are the main rewards?'. (6)

14 Calculated risks

Risks in business (and in life) are unavoidable. Well-run firms think about the risks that may turn against them, then estimate the possible impact. For example, the cost of dropping out of the Premiership is said to be about £20 million. Apart from the top five sides, each of the other clubs will think about the chance of relegation and the cost. If there are 3 relegation places for 15 teams, there is a 20 per cent chance of relegation *every year*. So a wise club chairman would have a plan for how the team would cope. Sadly, the past experience of teams such as Sheffield Wednesday and Nottingham Forest suggests that not every club does this.

Upside risk

Of course, luck does not have to be bad. New products can prove to be unexpected successes. New clubs can get great launch publicity and never look back. No one expected the first Harry Potter to be a worldwide smash – even the publisher, Bloomsbury Press. In 1995 Bloomsbury made a loss of £391,000. It offered an advance of £2500 for a 'quirky little book' called *Harry Potter and the Philosopher's Stone*. Today, author J. K. Rowling is one of the richest women in Britain and Bloomsbury Press will make a profit of £20 million in 2005/6.

Ideally, firms should plan for the unexpected ups as well as downs. The most obvious reason is to help cope with the success. High sales may be an embarrassment if you cannot keep up with them. The **Sony PSP**'s launch in Britain was put back by six months because demand was higher than expected in America and Japan. Sweetshops that run out of ice cream on hot days not only lose an opportunity to sell, but may also cause the customer to go somewhere else next time.

Calculating risks

There are two elements to risk:

1. What is the chance of it happening?
2. What is the cost of it happening?

> 'Take calculated risks. That is quite different from being rash'.
> General Patton, famous soldier

> 'If you do it right 51 per cent of the time you will end up a hero.'
> Alfred Sloan, president, General Motors

Big firms, such as **Nestlé** or **Johnson & Johnson**, know that only one in five new products is successful. So four out of every five (80 per cent) are flops. Yet companies such as Johnson & Johnson are constantly launching new products, backed by expensive TV advertising. Why? They do it because, on average, it takes them five new product launches for every success. They know that a flop will cost them around £10 million. A success, however, can easily bring in £50–100 million. So four flops costing £40 million are outweighed by one star product. That's intelligent, calculated risk. Here, the rewards outweigh the risks, so the risk:reward ratio is favourable.

For new businesses, life is much tougher. New firms will not know the chances of success or failure in their particular business; and will not know the costs involved. So new, small firms find it much harder to calculate risk and reward.

Drawing the right conclusions

> 'The policy of being too cautious is the greatest risk of all.'
> J. Nehru, India's first prime minister

For a small firm there is more to consider than just risk and reward. There are also the consequences. When Bloomsbury risked a £2500 advance to J. K. Rowling, it was not going to break the bank, even if Harry Potter proved a flop. But if a small firm takes a big step, failure may drag the business down. This is what happened to **EUJet** in 2005, when its move from Ireland to Kent created so many extra costs that the whole business was dragged under.

Clearly it is vital to think not only about the chance of something going wrong, but also the consequences. **Microsoft** can risk £100 million on a technology that may or may not work. £100 million is only 2 per cent of the money it keeps in its bank account. For a small firm, risking £10,000 may be risking the whole future of the business.

Clever businesspeople therefore try to weigh up:

- the chances of success or failure
- the costs or benefits of success or failure
- the implications for the business as a whole.

Exercises

(A and B: 20 marks; 25 minutes)

A Read the unit, then ask yourself:

1 Outline two significant risks that might be faced over the coming year by a small sports shop in your local high street. (4)
2 Explain why a firm should benefit from calculating the risks involved in its operations. (4)
3 Only 1 in 20 newly published books becomes a sales success. How does the experience of Bloomsbury Press explain why new books keep getting published? (5)

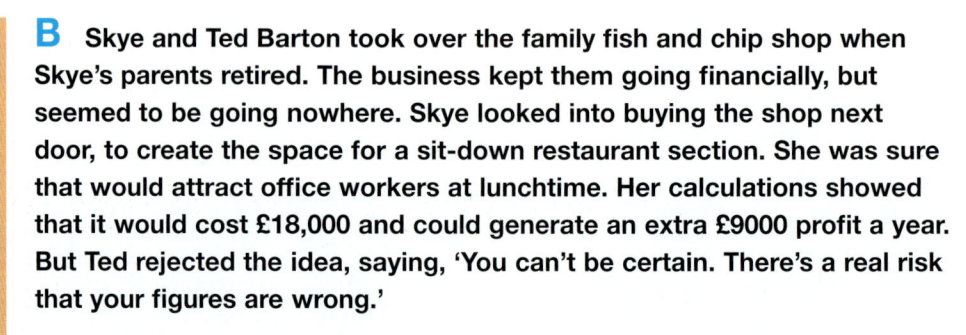

B Skye and Ted Barton took over the family fish and chip shop when Skye's parents retired. The business kept them going financially, but seemed to be going nowhere. Skye looked into buying the shop next door, to create the space for a sit-down restaurant section. She was sure that would attract office workers at lunchtime. Her calculations showed that it would cost £18,000 and could generate an extra £9000 profit a year. But Ted rejected the idea, saying, 'You can't be certain. There's a real risk that your figures are wrong.'

1 Describe Ted's attitude to risk. (3)
2 Explain why it is necessary for all businesspeople to be willing to take risks. (4)

Practice questions (20 marks; 25 minutes)

Allan Leighton, former boss of Asda, on risk

My definition of 'business risk' is some activity you're prepared to take to push the business forward with a pretty good chance of success.

My style is probably high risk. But under my criteria I have always approached it as a calculated gamble. The most important thing is that businesses won't grow without taking risks. But you can reduce that risk. That's in the quality of the planning and how well it's carried out.

What kills business is complacent staff. Complacency is always the greatest risk. That's why people get it wrong. What happens with complacency is, one, you get further away from the customer; two, you get further away from your people.
You have to stay very close to the customer and your people. The people who tell you it first are the customers... If you listen to the customer, you'll see if you are getting complacent or not. You've got to find ways of doing that.

(Source: adapted from questions posed by Pamela Shimell, author of *The Universe of Risk*, www.pearson.com)

Questions

1 a) Why may it be 'that businesses won't grow without taking risks'? (4)
  b) Why might 'complacency' be a risk? (3)
2 Explain how Allan Leighton's thoughts on risk compare with the quote in the text (see page 57) from Nehru, former prime minister of India. (5)
3 a) Outline two benefits of staying 'very close to the customer'. (4)
  b) Allan Leighton is clear that risk is not just about decisions, but also about how well they are carried out. How may it help if the boss stays close to staff ('your people') as well as to customers? (4)

15 Other enterprise qualities

To be enterprising requires more than creativity and a taste for risk. An enterprising individual is one who can:

1. Think ahead.
2. Make connections.
3. Show initiative.
4. Make decisions.
5. Show leadership.

Think ahead

> 'The only thing we know about the future is that it's going to be different.'
> Peter Drucker, management guru

There are two main parts to thinking ahead. The first is to be able to see what people will want in the future. On 2 September 2005 **HMV** announced the launch of a music download service (charging 79p per digital song). Coming three years after the launch of **Apple**'s massively successful iTunes service, the HMV boss admitted the company had moved too slowly. He said, 'We were unsure whether the digital delivery of music would become a viable and worthwhile market.' Not much evidence of enterprise there, then.

The second part of thinking ahead is to anticipate problems or opportunities. In autumn 2005 Daniel Reilly (Liverpool to the Canaries) and Martin Halstead (Oxford to Cambridge) were both about to launch their airlines. Yet the New Orleans hurricane had pushed aircraft fuel oil prices up to record levels. Had they thought about what they might do if the oil price jumped? Certainly they should have, because fuel is one of the biggest operating costs for airlines.

Make connections

In business, one thing leads to another. To have an idea of how everything connects together is vital. For instance, having the Olympics in London in 2012 has huge implications for many firms, especially in the hotel trade. The enterprising hotel manager must think ahead. How

SECTION 2 Showing enterprise

Olympics 2012

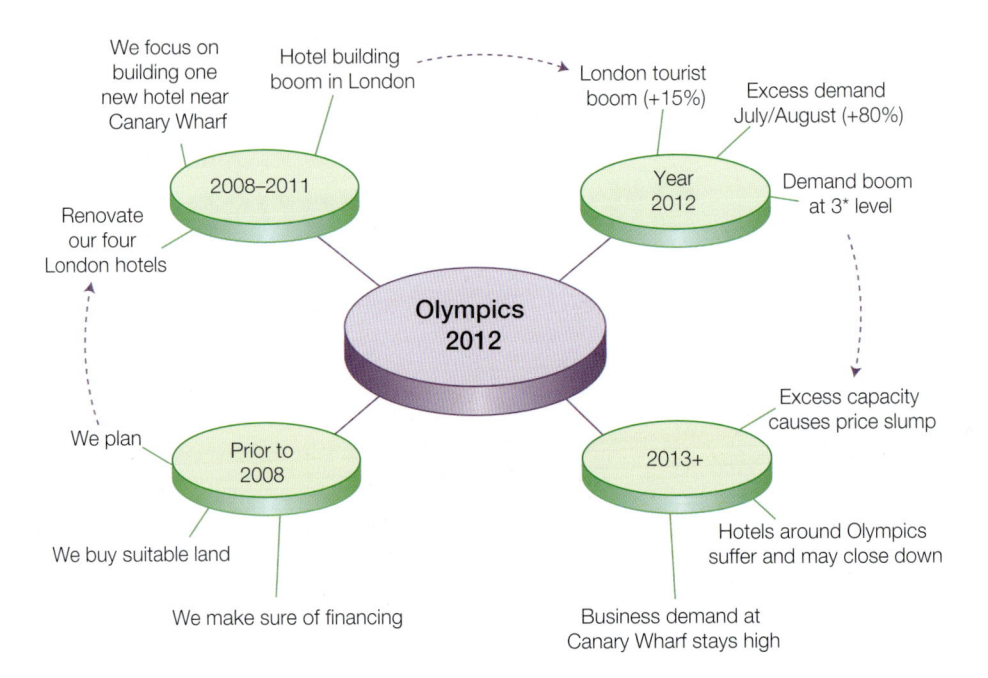

- **2008–2011**: We focus on building one new hotel near Canary Wharf; Hotel building boom in London
- **Year 2012**: London tourist boom (+15%); Excess demand July/August (+80%); Demand boom at 3* level
- **2013+**: Excess capacity causes price slump; Hotels around Olympics suffer and may close down; Business demand at Canary Wharf stays high
- **Prior to 2008**: Renovate our four London hotels; We plan; We buy suitable land; We make sure of financing

A small London hotel chain, thinking ahead to the Olympics 2012

will 2012 be? What will need to be done beforehand? What might life be like afterwards? After the 2004 Olympics, Athens was left with too many new hotels in the wrong location for tourists and business travellers.

A useful approach is to draw up a mind map. This encourages you to think about the option, and about how things link together. The figure above shows a mind map for a small London hotel chain, thinking ahead to the Olympics. It would be a way to think about the whole picture.

Show initiative

Initiative is crucial. It means not waiting for orders or until you see what everyone else is doing. It requires you to be bold, decisive and willing to accept that you might get it wrong. The initiative might not be as huge as Apple's move into the phone business with its iPhone. Here are other good examples of initiative.

- Cadbury's market research manager uses a large part of her budget to explore customer opinions of white chocolate-based face creams; if a successful new product emerges, she will be the hero; if not, the company may start to doubt her judgement.
- Jamie Oliver's initiative in approaching Greenwich council to get permission to carry out his school dinners experiment.

Only through initiative can a business hope to be first into a market; and only by being first do you have a chance to make a real impact.

Make decisions

'Ever notice that "What the hell" is always the right decision?'
Marilyn Monroe, film star

Decision making is crucial; not only when initiative could be taken, but also in response to difficulties. A hairdressers with three outlets may have one that is losing money. Decisions are required. Perhaps the outlet should close or perhaps it needs a revamp. When the bankrupt bookstore chain **Dillons** was taken over by **Waterstones**, over half the shops were found to have been losing money for years. But no one did anything about it!

To make decisions successfully, the key is to find out as much information as possible, from as many sources as possible. Most important are your staff and your customers. Ask for views and opinions, then decide, and carry the decision through without hesitation.

At the end of August 2005 Newcastle United FC was in disarray, having taken just one point from their first four games. The board had two choices: sack manager Graeme Souness or back him with money to buy better players. Within a week, the club spent more than £25 million on Owen, Solano and Luque. The decision was clear (though was to prove incorrect).

Show leadership

'A leader is a dealer in hope.'
Napoleon Bonaparte, soldier and French emperor

Leadership has a lot to do with qualities such as decisiveness, initiative and the ability to think ahead. One more element, though, is the personality and the character to make people believe in you. This might be helped by self-confidence, but in fact some excellent leaders are quite shy. Some are great at one-to-one chats, but less comfortable when speaking in public or when chatting in a group of people. Although Richard Branson comes over very well on TV, he is said to be very shy and often tongue-tied.

Good leadership needs to be based on good judgement about the right decision or initiative, plus the determination to see things through. It also requires an ability to make people want to share the leader's path (i.e. to help achieve his or her aims). This requires either charisma or the ability to make people respect and believe in him or her.

Unit 15 Other enterprise qualities

Different leadership approaches

Leader	Approach to leadership	Outcome
Alex Ferguson	Tough, almost bullying; very decisive; brutally honest.	Gains huge respect from staff.
Richard Branson	Full of initiative; friendly and sociable; inspirational.	Love and respect from staff.
Tony Blair	Decisive; persuasive; claims to listen, but seems not to hear.	Gets what he wants, but results can be divisive.

Exercises

(A and B: 25 marks; 30 minutes)

A Read the unit, then ask yourself:

1 Explain how a business can benefit from a leader who thinks ahead. (3)
2 If you were the boss of a company, outline two actions you could take that would encourage staff to show more initiative. (4)
3 Looking back to August 2005, did the Newcastle board make the right decision? Briefly explain your answer. (3)
4 Outline one strength and one weakness of your own which would affect your ability to be a successful leader. (4)

B Joy Marsh, boss of a small advertising agency, was worried about the effect of rising expense account spending. When she asked her staff, they were equally puzzled about the possible cause. At a board meeting a director mentioned production quality problems since the head TV producer had left the agency. Joy then spent two days with the TV production team, to try to understand the issues. This made her realise that staff were spending more on their expense accounts to give posh lunches to unhappy clients. She solved the problems within a week by hiring a top producer from New York.

1 a) Outline the connections Joy made. (3)
   b) Explain the benefit to the business of making those connections. (4)
2 Outline two leadership qualities shown by Joy. (4)

Practice questions (20 marks; 25 minutes)

COOL DINNERS

Jamie Oliver, celebrity chef, took the initiative to alter the diets of nearly 30,000 school kids in Greenwich. He soon found three massive problems: a budget of only 37p per meal, the fact that most 'dinner ladies' could not cook, and that many school 'kitchens' only had equipment for reheating food. Then came the biggest problem of all: that the pupils did not want freshly cooked, inventive food. They had grown up with fat-laden foods such as Turkey Twizzlers and chips, and did not want to change.

From *The Guardian*, Tuesday 15 February 2005:

There were times when Oliver felt like giving up. 'I'd be getting hassles with the contractors, hassles with the school, hassle with the kids and hassle with the council', he remembers. 'The responsibility felt enormous. It was like everything was down to me and I had to reassure everyone that it was going to be fine, when inside I felt like a sack of shit.'

But gradually everything fell into place. The menus worked out, and the processed food was consigned to history. A contract for proper meat was negotiated with Harvey Nichols, retailer to the rich and famous, which worked out cheaper than the previous one for processed chunks with a wholesaler and, biggest achievement of all, the kids started eating Jamie's food. 'It was a close-run thing', he says. 'When we first abandoned the processed food, most of the kids abandoned us. It was only when we had a spell of really nasty weather and the kids couldn't be bothered to go elsewhere that they started coming back.'

Questions

1 a) Outline three enterprise qualities shown by Jamie Oliver. (6)
  b) Which one of these qualities do you think was the most important in his success in this case? Explain why. (5)
2 Jamie managed to keep going when times were tough. How important do you think determination might be in a successful leader? (4)
3 Outline the evidence in the text about the satisfaction Jamie gained from his school dinners initiative. (5)

SECTION 3

PUTTING A BUSINESS IDEA INTO PRACTICE

16 Introduction to getting it right

In spring 2004 Trevor and Ray started a company making and selling high-quality garden furniture. Although young, they had more than ten years' experience between them in this business, and had spotted a gap in the £500 to £1000 price range. They would sell directly from a website, advertised in garden centres and gardening magazines. The business was based in their home town of Carlisle.

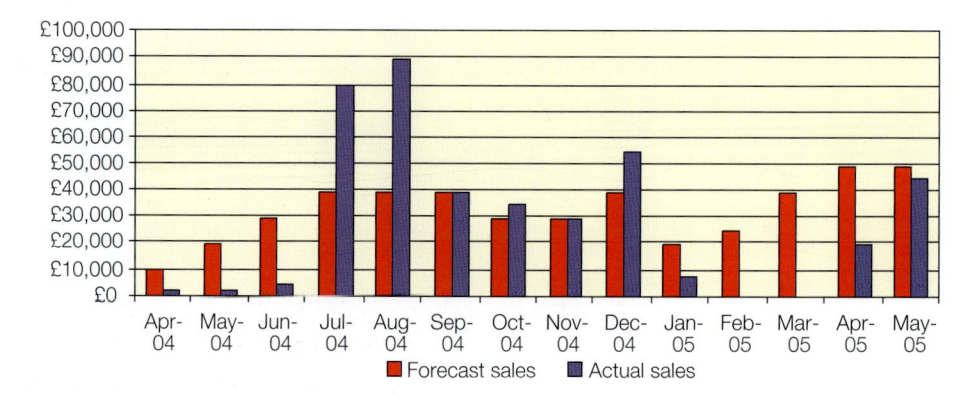

Sales of Trevor and Ray's garden furniture

Before starting, they estimated the sales they would achieve and all the costs involved, month by month. They used these figures to get a bank loan to help provide the £48,000 it cost them to start up. As the bar chart above shows, the early months were a struggle, but after the 'terrific quality furniture' was mentioned in a BBC TV gardening programme, sales went crazy in July.

Trevor and Ray had to hire 12 extra carpenters to match production to the level of demand. They only hired 3 permanently, with the rest on weekly contracts. This was fortunate because in January 2005 Carlisle was put under four feet of water by flooding and the factory was ruined. It took three months to start up again. Several other local businesses closed and never reopened. Trevor and Ray had made sure the previous summer to treat their July/August boom as a lucky windfall. They banked the **profit** rather than spent it, and were able to use that money to rebuild the business after the floods.

From business idea to business success

Many new businesses fail. No one is sure of the right figures, but probably no more than half are successful. In many cases this is because too little thought has gone into it. People start up second-hand bookshops or little teashops because they want to. Husband and wife may agree, 'It would be lovely to run our own bookshop'. In fact, it may prove quite depressing to run a bookshop if hardly anyone comes in.

In other cases people may have a great business idea. They may have thought it through with care and intelligence. Yet the business may flop. Good ideas do not automatically become great successes. This is because many businesses are complicated to run effectively. For example, to start up and run a restaurant effectively, you have to:

1. Find a great location.
2. Negotiate an affordable rent.
3. Design a stylish restaurant and a workmanlike kitchen.
4. Get it built, equipped and decorated on time and not too expensively.
5. Appoint high quality, well-motivated staff.
6. Train them well and keep them motivated.
7. Agree the right menus to appeal to the customers you want.
8. Set prices at the right balance between customer 'value' and your own profit.
9. Keep ordering the right quantity and quality of supplies (meat, fish etc.).
10. Keep the atmosphere in the restaurant as lively and enjoyable as possible.
11. Make sure that every customer receives fresh, hot food without long waits between courses.

And so on and so on, lunchtime and evening, every week for 52 weeks a year. One bad experience may mean a customer never returns; and if that customer is a restaurant reviewer, he or she may turn hundreds of people away from the restaurant. The following quotes from national newspaper restaurant reviews in 2005 and 2006 demonstrate the point (both about restaurants charging £90 to £100 for a meal for two):

> 'The potato was so grossly oversalted you'd be reported to social services if you fed it to a three-year-old.'

> 'Sliced bread turned up warm on the outside and frozen in the middle. The second lot was still stone cold in the middle and the end piece was hard and stale.'

Success requires a clear plan, enthusiastic leadership, effective organisation and a bit of luck. It starts with a realistic forecast of sales. How many customers are likely? And how much will they be prepared to pay? A clothes shop might attract 400 visitors on a Saturday, but only 50 may buy something, perhaps with an average value of £20. The Saturday takings may seem great at £20 × 50 = £1000, but what if the clothes cost £500 to buy, the wage bill is £250 and other bills amount to £150? With costs of £500+£250+£150=£900, there is only £100 profit on the Saturday. The theft of just one expensive dress might wipe that out.

So a sales forecast must be compared with the costs to make an estimate of the profit. If the profit seems too low, the entrepreneur should think how to boost it. Should prices be increased? Or should costs be reduced? Or should a different location be found to attract more customers? The thing to avoid is to start a business and only realise later that it never had much chance of success. For example, Stelios, the founder of **easyJet**, launched a chain of internet cafes called **easyInternetcafé**. He later closed many of them down because the amount charged per hour could not cover the costs of the business.

Financing the start-up

Having worked out a profitable business idea and set out a believable forecast of **revenues** and costs, it is time to raise the capital to start the business. The key to persuading others is for them to be sure that you are backing the idea with as much money as you can. No lender would provide more than half the launch capital. They want the entrepreneur to have risked at least half the start-up capital. And lenders are sure to want security for their money. In other words, they want their money backed by specific assets, such as property. If the business fails, the bank seizes the assets that are the security on its investment. The entrepreneur may lose her/his whole investment, but the bank will probably be okay.

Although financing the start-up can be difficult, the rewards may be huge. **Skype** was started in 2003 by two Swedish engineers. This quickly became the top name in internet telephone systems and in October 2005 was bought by **eBay** for an incredible $2.5 **billion**.

As shown in the table below, although every company has share capital, not all have borrowings. Those that do tend to use the flexibility of a bank overdraft in preference to the rigidity of a bank loan. Very few receive any form of government grant/allowance to help in the process of starting up.

Sources of finance for small companies in Britain

Share capital	100%
Overdraft	53%
Leasing	27%
Medium-term loans	24%
Grants	6%

(Source: Finance for SMEs, University of Warwick, 2005)

Conclusion

To start a successful business requires a great idea and a great plan for making it happen. A good understanding of finance is important, because profit can only happen if costs are kept below the value of the sales. Investors demand the opportunity to make good profits. So business leaders have to know how to build a good level of sales, and how to keep costs down. In a business such as **Ryanair**, this is part of the everyday thinking of every manager. No wonder Ryanair has been such a success.

Revision essentials

Billion: one thousand million (1,000,000,000).
Profit: revenue minus costs. This is the surplus that can be used to reward shareholders or to invest in the expansion of the business.
Revenue: the value of sales (i.e. the number of customers × the average amount they spend). This does not allow for costs.

Exercises

(25 marks; 30 minutes)

Read the unit, then ask yourself:

1. Look at the sales graph for Trevor and Ray's business. Then calculate:
   a) the extra sales in August 2004, when comparing actual with forecast figures (2)
   b) the sales shortfall in April 2005, when comparing actual with forecast sales (2)
   c) the approximate total sales lost because of the flooding. Show your workings and explain your reasoning. (5)

2. a) Reread the 11 steps identified for setting up a successful restaurant. Identify six steps to setting up a successful clothes shop. (6)
   b) Explain which two you consider the most important and why. (4)
   c) Outline two ways in which luck might affect whether or not a new clothes shop is successful. (4)

3. Outline one reason why a bank insists on its loans being backed by security. (2)

Practice questions

(20 marks; 25 minutes)

For many years British Airways and Virgin Atlantic have made a high proportion of all their profits from flying business-class passengers on the London–New York route. Return ticket prices are as high as £4500, even though an economy ticket costs just £299.

Given the success of easyJet and Ryanair in Europe, it was no surprise to hear that a brand new airline was starting up to offer business-only flights from London to New York. Eos, set up by a former executive at British Airways, would be offering return fares for £2500. The flat-bed seats would be bigger than BA's and would have an extra seat available for business chats on board. Boeing 757 aircraft would have their 200 seats cut down to just 48 for the Eos service.

A shock awaited Eos, though. No sooner had the publicity campaign been launched when a second all-business airline was announced. MAXjet would be pricing its return trips at £850, for which a passenger would get plenty of space, though not quite a flat bed.

The first Eos flight took place in October 2005 and MAXjet followed up in November. A *Times* journalist travelled on both, concluding that MAXjet 'beats Eos hands down for value'. Both airlines have kept quite quiet about how well they have been doing, but MAXjet's January 2006 newspaper advertisements for return tickets at £599 suggested difficulties filling the planes.

Questions

1. Outline two ways in which Eos could market itself to British Airways' business-class customers. (4)
2. Why should Eos be especially concerned that it was beaten 'hands down for value' by MAXjet? (5)
3. It seems bad luck for Eos that MAXjet had the same idea. Explain two possible effects on Eos of the unplanned arrival of a competitor. (4)
4. In a year or two's time these airlines may be winning a lot of market share from British Airways and Virgin. Discuss how BA and Virgin might respond to the threat of serious competition. (7)

17 Estimating revenue

Ted Draycott's alarm goes off at 3.45 every morning. He drives from Watford to Covent Garden market to buy the best and freshest fruit and vegetables. If strawberries are 32p a punnet and the weather forecast is good, he might buy 4 dozen boxes (nearly 1000 punnets). He expects to sell them on for 45p, so that Watford's greengrocers can charge the public 95p or £1. If the buying price is 50p he might buy only a dozen boxes, especially if rain is forecast.

Ted's skill is an ability to make quick, accurate **sales forecasts**. If he gets things wrong he may run out of strawberries halfway round the town, leaving some of his greengrocer customers angry. Or he might buy too many and find himself pleading with people to take the fruit off his hands, perhaps at a cut-down price.

On a good day, Ted can make £800 profit between 3.45 and 10.45 a.m., leaving himself free all afternoon and evening. On a bad day he may take 12 hours to barely cover his costs. In fact, his profit averages £2000+ a week, so you can see that he's doing pretty well!

For a bigger business, such as **Innocent Drinks**, there needs to be a bit more certainty. If Ted has a bad week, he can cut down, to stop spending too much. Innocent employs over 50 people and has a wage bill of £40,000 a week. It simply cannot afford to have weeks where no money is made or where revenues are expected, but do not turn up. Nor will **Tesco** accept, 'Sorry, we haven't any strawberry smoothies this week; there's been a rush on them and we've run out.' Every business needs to find a way to estimate **sales revenue**.

Sales revenue comes from the number of things you sell multiplied by the price you charge. If Yeovil Town FC sells 7000 tickets at £20 each, its revenue is £140,000. Yeovil decides its own ticket price, so the uncertain factor is the level of demand. Will it sell 7000 tickets (£140,000) or 5500 tickets (£110,000)? Even for such a well-run club, the difference of £30,000 is very important.

Price

For some businesses the price cannot be estimated with full confidence. At the start of 2005, **BP** might have expected that its petrol pump price would average 85p per litre. In fact, it proved to be nearer to 95p. In Africa, farmers producing coffee could have hoped for a price of 60p a kilo in 2002, but by 2004 they were receiving only 35p. The 40 per cent fall in their incomes condemned them to desperately low living standards.

Prices cannot be estimated with confidence when:

- the business operates in a market where prices change in the short term due to variations in supply and demand
- competition is direct and fierce (e.g. Ryanair competing with easyJet)
- you are launching a new product and cannot be sure of the consumer response (e.g. the original Xbox launched at $399, but the price was cut to $299 within a few weeks).

Quantity

Occasionally, the demand for a product or service can be judged with confidence. Robbie Williams concert tours have always sold out, so it seems safe to expect them to sell out next time round (but what about Michael Jackson?). Similarly, sales of **Heinz** baked beans are extremely predictable. They will have seasonal peaks and troughs (sell more in the autumn and winter), but Heinz managers know that, so they will be able to forecast with a high degree of accuracy. The precision of the revenue estimate will be helped by the strength of the brand. Not even Tesco could decide to stop stocking Heinz beans; nor could a huge advertising campaign for **HP** beans hurt Heinz. A revenue forecast made for six months' time by a Heinz director would prove very accurate. Therefore the business can make sure it has the right quantity of machinery, staff and raw ingredients. Managing this type of business is easy.

It is quite different when trying to plan the revenues for a posh London restaurant. Customers will usually be a mixture of wealthy Londoners, businesspeople and visitors to London. The restaurant could be full this week, but in six months it might have been emptied by:

- a newspaper review that condemns it as dull and overpriced
- an economic slowdown, leading to cutbacks in luxury spending
- terrorism or other reasons for people to avoid London.

Conclusion

The point can be summed up in this way: revenue is the quantity of sales multiplied by the price. In some cases this is easy to predict; in many other cases it is virtually impossible. For every business the circumstances are different. This affects the ability of the firm to run smoothly and efficiently. Most managers would rather have a stable revenue of £1 million a month than a revenue that averages £1.2 million, but in an erratic way. This is because predictable revenues allow firms to keep costs low enough to make a good profit. Revenues that jump around make it much harder to trade profitably.

Revision essentials
Sales forecasts: estimates of the future level of sales to be achieved by a new or existing product.
Sales revenue: the total value of sales made within a period of time, such as a month. To find the value, multiply the quantity sold by the price.

Exercises   (30 marks; 30 minutes)

Read the unit, then ask yourself:

1. **a)** What is the formula for calculating a company's sales revenue? (2)
   b) If a bus company sold 4000 tickets a day at £1.20 each, what would be its daily sales revenue? (2)
   c) If you knew that selling 500 shirts produced a revenue of £7500, what would be the price per shirt? (3)
2. Explain briefly whether it would be easy or hard to predict next year's selling price for:
   a) Cadbury Dairy Milk chocolate (3)
   b) the world price for oil. (3)
3. Why may direct and fierce competition make it difficult to estimate prices with confidence? (3)
4. Outline two ways in which a business could use accurate forecasts of future sales. (6)
5. Give two reasons why a revenue forecast made for six months' time by a Heinz director would prove very accurate. (2)
6. Explain briefly whether it would be easy or hard to predict next year's sales volumes for:
   a) Topshop clothes (3)
   b) *The Sun* newspaper. (3)

Practice questions (20 marks; 20 minutes)

Xbox 360 sales start slow in Japan

Microsoft's Xbox 360 game console has got off to a slow start in Japan, with sales of only 62,135 Xbox 360 consoles over the weekend. This figure represents just 39 per cent of the 159,000 machines that were available for the Japanese launch.

Microsoft has struggled to penetrate the Japanese market, traditionally dominated by local rivals Sony and Nintendo. Sony's share of the Japanese console market is estimated to be about 80 per cent, compared with less than 5 per cent for Microsoft.

The original Xbox sold about 123,000 units in the first three days of its launch in 2002. But with Sony expected to launch the PlayStation 3 next spring, Microsoft was hoping that the early release date of the 360 would give it a clear advantage over its biggest rival. However, these sales figures will be a big disappointment to the US software giant.

The 360 costs 39,795 yen ($330) in Japan, cheaper than the comparable package in the US, where it sells for about $400.

(Source: **Nick Gibbens**, 13 December 2005, 999today.com, sales data from Enterbrain)

Questions

1 a) Microsoft seems to have overestimated the demand for its Xbox 360 in Japan. Outline two possible reasons for this overestimate. (4)

b) If Microsoft had known how weak the demand was going to be in Japan, the company could have directed more products to Britain, where it ran out of stock. Examine two possible effects on the company of its failure to meet the high demand in Britain. (6)

2 a) Why may Microsoft have decided to price the new Xbox at $330 in Japan compared with $400 in America? (3)

b) What revenue was generated in Japan from the first weekend's sales of 62,135 consoles? Give your answer in dollars. (3)

3 Outline two actions Microsoft might take to strengthen the sales position of Xbox in Japan before the launch of the Sony PlayStation 3 the following spring. (4)

18 Estimating costs

The costs of making potato crisps

What do you think it would cost to start up a business making potato crisps? After all, the attractions are clear. A bag of **Walkers** selling for 35p weighs only 30 g. As potatoes can be bought for 33p a kilo, the potato inside the bag costs about 1p. There's oil, salt and flavourings as well, but not conceivably coming to more than 2p in total. If the packaging materials cost another 1p in total, our 35p bag cost 3p to make. No wonder Gary Lineker looks so pleased with himself.

Of course, it is not that simple. There are many other costs: the factory rent, the cost of machinery, the salaries of the research and development staff who think up the new flavours, and the marketing people who plan the advertising and promotions.

For someone thinking of starting their own business, estimating costs is one of the hardest things to do. The starting point is to realise that there are two types of cost: **fixed costs** and **variable costs**.

Variable costs

These are costs that vary with the quantity sold and therefore the quantity made. They are costs that relate directly to making the sale and therefore making the product. If Walkers runs a brilliant new advertising campaign and crisp sales double, they will have to buy in twice as many potatoes, twice as much packaging, and so on. These are variable costs. They rise and fall in relation to sales and therefore output.

Examples of variable costs include:

- **raw materials** (e.g. potatoes for making crisps; cocoa beans for making chocolate)
- **bought-in components** (e.g. spark plugs for making cars; headphones when making iPods)
- **energy** used in the production process (e.g. gas for cooking in a restaurant)
- **piece-rate labour**, which means paying people per unit of work, e.g. £2 per pair of jeans made; commission paid to sales staff would also be a variable cost.

Fixed costs

These costs do not change as output changes. They are fixed in relation to output. Take the rent on a clothes shop, for example – it must be paid, whether sales are terrific or awful. Therefore it is fixed. Note, though, that the landlord can put up your rent, so the fact that it is a fixed cost does not mean it never changes.

Fixed costs are often related to a time period rather than sales or output. Rent, for instance, might be paid per month, as might staff salaries.

Examples of fixed costs include:

- **salaries** of permanent staff
- **rent and (council) rates**
- **marketing spending** (the budget for this will be set at the start of the year, and will not rise just because sales rise)
- **machinery and equipment**, which might include delivery vans.

Stop and think, what are the fixed costs and what are the variable costs of running:

- A Topshop branch?
- Manchester United FC?
- A kebab shop?

Then look at the answers in the table opposite.

SECTION 3 Putting a business idea into practice

Separating fixed and variable costs

TYPE OF BUSINESS	FIXED COSTS	VARIABLE COSTS
A Topshop branch	Rent and rates	Buying clothes from suppliers
	Staff wages and salaries	Carrier bags
	Security and insurance costs	Damage/wastage/theft (which
	Lighting and heating	rise and fall depending
	Regular redecoration	on how busy the shop is)
Manchester United FC	Players' wages	Programme and ticket printing
	Staff salaries	Cost of pies/food bought in
	Ground maintenance	Cost of beer/drinks bought in
A kebab shop	Rent and rates	Buying in the meat, bread,
	Staff wages and salaries	salad, potatoes (or
	Lighting and heating	frozen chips)
	Insurance costs	Energy (gas etc.) for cooking
	Irregular redecoration	Paper bags and other packaging

Getting the numbers right

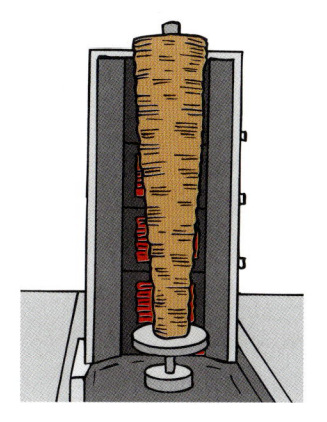

If you plan to open a kebab shop, it may be easy to decide which are the variable and which are the fixed costs, but what will the *exact* figures be? The only way to find out is to work at it. A trip to a local estate agent will tell you what rents are likely at different parts of the high street (they might vary from £600 to £4000 a month, depending on location). The estate agent will also know the level of council tax/rates on different properties. A look in the jobs advertisements in the local paper will show the hourly pay rates and salary levels locally. A few phone calls to insurance companies will give an idea of the insurance costs. A builder could give a quote on the cost of turning the shell of an empty shop into a kebab shop, with the electrics, gas and water in the right places. So most of the fixed costs can be established fairly easily.

It may be harder to estimate the variable costs. A Google search would get you the names of doner kebab meat suppliers. (I have just done this, and learned that a doner kebab grill/display machine costs between £650 and £1005. From a phone call I have been offered kebab meat to make 450 kebabs for £135 – that's 30p per kebab!) Of course, without experience you cannot be sure that you would really get 450 portions from the meat; so a sensible businessperson would be very cautious in estimating costs. To be on the safe side I would allow 60p in meat variable costs (plus the cost of pitta bread, salad etc., so perhaps 80p in total).

Unit 18 Estimating costs

77

Having completed my research, I can estimate the following totals:

- fixed costs of the kebab shop: £1200 per week
- variable costs per kebab: £0.80.

I can now calculate the **total costs** at different levels of business. Most importantly, if I carry out research into potential sales levels, I can estimate the costs involved. For example, if research shows that 600 customers will come per week, my total weekly costs will be: 600 × £0.80 = £480 (variable costs) + £1200 (fixed costs) = £1680 (total costs). As long as the estimated revenues are higher than this figure, there is money to be made.

Revision essentials

Fixed costs: costs that do not change when sales/output changes.
Total costs: all the costs of making a specific level of sales (i.e. fixed costs plus total variable costs).
Variable costs: costs that change in direct proportion to changes in sales/output.

Exercises

(20 marks; 25 minutes)

Read the unit, then ask yourself:

1. Explain the difference between fixed costs and variable costs. (4)
2. A greengrocer buys punnets of strawberries for 50p and sells them for £1. She must also pay £120 in weekly rent and £180 for other fixed costs.
   a) What is the total cost of selling 500 punnets per week? (2)
   b) What is the total cost of selling 1000 punnets per week? (2)
3. Identify two fixed and two variable costs of running:
   a) a secondary school with 1200 pupils (4)
   b) a Tesco supermarket. (4)
4. Outline two reasons why people starting a new, small firm might make cost estimates that prove to be too low. (4)

Practice questions (25 marks; 25 minutes)

When the Choy Sum Chinese restaurant opened in Wimbledon, it was in a great position to estimate costs accurately. The owners already ran a Chinese five miles away in Fulham, so they knew how much to allow for the variable and fixed costs of their new outlet. Before opening, their plans showed:

Average price per dish	£4.40
Average variable cost per dish	£1.80
Fixed weekly overheads	£2000
Number of dishes sold p.w.	3000
Weekly revenue	£13,200

In fact, though, it proved harder than expected. The owners knew how much the ingredients *should* cost in a chicken and black bean sauce, but actual variable costs proved 25 per cent higher. The owners checked the figures carefully, trying to find whether staff were stealing food from the kitchens.

The explanation came in two parts. First, the restaurant manager at Wimbledon failed to attract and keep good chefs. So customers sent poor-quality dishes back to the kitchen and the cooking had to be redone. The second problem stemmed from the first. Bookings were slow, with only 200 customers buying 1000 dishes per week, so fresh food went off and had to be thrown away.

Questions

1. If the forecast of 3000 dishes per week had been met, what would have been the total costs of operating Choy Sum, Wimbledon? (4)
2. Explain why sales proved lower than expected. (4)
3. Actual variable costs were 25 per cent higher than predicted; and the number of dishes sold was only 1000. What were the total costs of the business? How does that figure compare with the revenue generated from 1000 dishes sold? (6)
4. Identify two likely variable costs and three likely fixed costs of operating a Chinese restaurant. (5)
5. Choy Sum restaurant has now closed down in Wimbledon. To what extent can its failure be blamed on the owners' sloppy approach to estimating costs? (6)

Unit 18 Estimating costs

19 Calculating and using profit

Profit is the difference between revenue and costs. It is calculated by the formula: **revenue minus total costs = profit**. If costs are greater than revenue, the result would be a negative number. That means making a loss.

Look at the position of **British Airways**. In 2002 it had a bad year and made a loss of £100 million. In 2005 its position was much better and it made a profit of £500 million.

British Airways' operating costs and profit, 2002 and 2005

	2002	2005
Revenue	£8300m	£7800m
Operating costs	£8400m	£7300m
Operating profit	−£100m	£500m

For new, small firms, profit can be very difficult to achieve in the early days. Costs may be higher than necessary because staff have not yet learned to do things efficiently. Revenues may be low because word has not yet spread about the quality of the service you offer. W. H. Hales, a shop supplying and engraving sports trophies, took five years to become profitable. That was because it took that long for the word about the shop to spread among local football teams.

Forecasting profit

Unit 17 explained about estimating revenue, and Unit 18 showed how to estimate costs. Profit forecasts put these two estimates together. For a brand new firm it will be especially important that the forecast is done cautiously. In other words, cost estimates should allow for unexpectedly high figures; revenue estimates should allow for disappointing figures. If you start off with a gloomy forecast, the surprises should all be pleasing ones.

In this case, shown in the chart below, a new pizza takeaway business, Milano Pizza, had forecast a loss in its first year. It only expected to make a profit after 18 months of trading. In fact, it had a stroke of luck as the local **Pizza Hut** closed down! As a result, sales proved much higher than expected.

What is the effect of overoptimistic forecasting?

The problem with optimism is that disappointment can cause serious problems. If managers forecast a £90,000 profit, they might plan to use the money to launch a new product. Money will be spent on researching the market, and perhaps testing a new product. This might be wasted if low profits make it impossible to finance the product launch. So forecasting should be done cautiously.

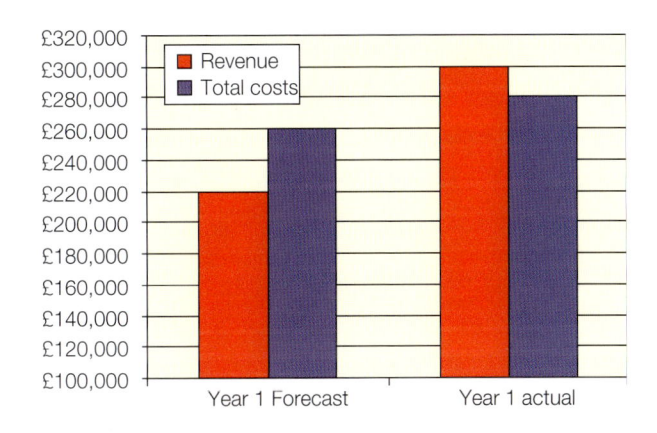

First year at Milano Pizza

Using profit

The word 'profit' tends to suggest riches. In fact, reinvested profit generates 60 per cent of all the money invested to help firms grow. In other words, most of the capital firms use to finance growth comes from their own profit. Among the typical uses of profit may be:

- to invest in extra property or machinery, to help the business grow
- to invest in more efficient systems or technology, to help cut costs
- to help fund extra stocks of materials or finished goods
- to pay out as dividends to shareholders, to give them an annual return on their investment.

The higher the profit, the easier it is to compete with the best firms around you. The best recruits want to go to the firms with the best prospects. High profits can help build a firm's reputation as a secure, attractive employer.

Dealing with losses

Business is not simple or predictable. A business that starts successfully may suffer a downturn in revenue if a new competitor opens up. Revenue may slip below costs, pushing the business into losses. This may not be too serious if it only lasts for a month or two, but lengthy periods of loss-making will force the closure of all but the richest businesses. To try to bring the business back into a profit-making position, the managers could:

- try to boost revenues, especially if this can be done without increasing costs, for example a price increase
- act to reduce variable costs per unit (e.g. talk to the workforce about why and how to reduce wastage, either in a factory or a shop)
- act to reduce fixed costs (e.g. consider moving to cheaper premises).

When considering how to cut losses, it is important to consider the effect each idea can have on the other factors. Cutting variable costs, for example, could damage sales if it is done by finding a cheaper, but lower quality, supplier.

Exercises

(A and B: 30 marks; 30 minutes)

A Read the unit, then ask yourself:

1. What is the difference between revenue and profit? (2)
2. Using the figures provided, briefly explain how British Airways turned a £100 million loss into a £500 million profit. (3)
3. Explain why, when making cost estimates, firms should allow for unexpectedly high figures. (3)
4. Look at the bar chart for Milano Pizza.
   a) Identify the forecast profit for year 1. (2)
   b) Identify the actual profit for year 1. (1)
   c) By how much did Milano Pizza's actual profit beat the forecast? (1)
5. After two difficult years since starting the business, Mark and Sima's coffee bar has made £8000 profit in the third year. Identify three possible ways this profit might be used by the business. (3)

B Toni's ice cream van sells 150 ice creams a day at £1 each. The variable costs are 20p per ice cream and the fixed costs of running the van are £50 a day.

1 What is Toni's profit per day? (4)

2 Toni's daughter wants him to put the price up to £1.20; she thinks sales will stay at 150 ice creams, but Toni is worried that sales will fall to 125.

   a) By how much will Toni's profit change if his daughter is right? (4)

   c) What will be the new profit if Toni is right about the price rise to £1.20? (4)

   d) Outline one reason why Toni might still want to keep the price at £1. (3)

20 The role and importance of cash

At the end of the year a business looks at its revenues and costs and works out the profit. Day by day, though, **cash** is more important than profit. Suppliers have to be paid, wages have to be paid, the rent and telephone bills have to be paid – with cash.

In business today the word 'cash' means more than the notes and coins in your pocket. Writing a cheque or paying by debit card is (just about) as quick as paying in banknotes, so it is regarded as the same thing. Whatever is in a firm's current account at the bank is just as useful as cash. Accountants use the term 'cash at bank' to summarise that it is the notes and coins you hold *plus* the money in your bank accounts. (From now on, when this book refers to cash, it always means 'cash at bank'.)

Why does cash matter?

Cash matters because, without it, bills go unpaid and a business can be taken to court and perhaps closed down. Staff expect to be paid every Friday, for example, and will not accept a boss saying, 'Sorry, I can't afford to pay you today. Hopefully we'll be okay on Monday.' Yet it is hard enough for individuals to *always* have cash available; if you are running a business with 15 staff and 150 customers, the problems are much greater.

On 10 September 2001 one British firm was celebrating winning a contract from a fourth major airline to supply it with steel cutlery. The following day's catastrophe at the Twin Towers in New York meant – worldwide – that all airlines were banned from using metal knives and forks. Overnight – and totally unpredictably – the firm's cash income dried up. It was spring 2005 before British airlines were allowed to begin using metal cutlery again. In the meantime the cutlery company had – somehow – to find the cash to keep going.

A FIRM'S POSSIBLE CASH PROBLEMS	CONSEQUENCES
Unable to pay the rent on time.	Landlord could evict you (e.g. you lose your prime-location shop premises).
Unable to pay staff reliably.	Your best staff find jobs elsewhere.
Unable to pay suppliers on time.	They may ignore you when they have some prime goods to sell (e.g. limited quantities of a hot new PS3 game).
Unable to seize a new business opportunity.	A close rival closes down and has stock available at knockdown prices, but you do not have the cash to buy it.

Problems managing cash

There are three factors that make it particularly hard to manage cash.

1. Seasonal sales, such as a toy shop with 50 per cent of the year's total sales in December. For many months of the year trading is so poor that costs are not covered, so cash totals go down and down; it may be a struggle to survive until next Christmas.

2. When you have a few large customers, if one of them fails to pay on time, your cash position is squeezed badly. In 2005 the Nippon Electric Glass factory in South Wales closed down because its main customer (Sony) stopped making TVs in its factory down the road.

3. When starting a business (e.g. if you are starting a restaurant there are huge start-up costs in the building and decoration, the kitchen equipment and the staff recruitment and training) cash can only start coming in when the doors open for the first time, but business may start slowly until reputation spreads by word of mouth. This creates a cash position such as that shown in the figure below. If the business started up with £300,000 of finance, any cost overruns in the building work could have pushed the business under before it had even started!

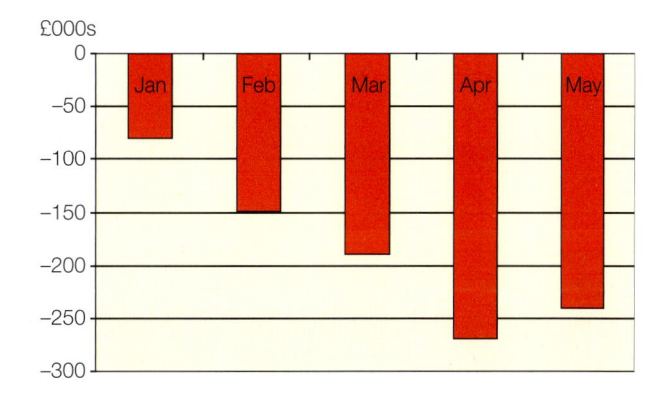

Cash position when opening a restaurant on 1 May

Unit 20 The role and importance of cash

How should cash be managed?

The key is to forecast the flows of cash into and out of the business. This topic (**cash flow**) is covered in the next unit. In addition to careful forecasting, a business must take care to:

- Negotiate a generous overdraft facility at the bank. A bank overdraft is a flexible way to borrow what you want, when you want and for how long you want. If you have no cash in your bank, but expect a fat cheque from a customer on Monday, you pay your £7000 salary bill today, Friday, using your overdraft. The cost of borrowing £7000 for three days would be less than £6 – well worth it to keep staff happy! Overdrafts (and other forms of borrowing) are explained fully in Unit 22: Raising finance.
- Keep costs under control; cash should never be a serious problem if the business is profitable (i.e. costs are lower than revenues). If business is poor, good managers make sure to cut costs – especially inessential ones such as staff mobile phones, expense accounts and renewing company cars.
- Keep the cash coming in. Most business in Britain is done on credit, not for cash. In other words, if Versace sells £400,000 worth of dresses to Harrods, the latter may be given two or three months to pay. A poorly run firm may be too soft on customers who fail to pay up on time. Firms allow customers an average of 70 days to pay up; but some firms allow over 120 days, which is four months! Waiting this long to be paid can strain a firm's cash resources and is no way to run a business.

Conclusion

Cash is the lifeblood of every business. Literally, without cash the business dies. Therefore it is vital to plan how much is needed and where to get it from. The best possible source is from your own customers – making sure they pay up on time. It is also necessary to allow for the unexpected, which is why a large overdraft facility is a vital resource. Ideally you would use it rarely, to keep interest charges down. But when it is needed, its flexibility takes the pressure out of difficult financial situations.

> **Revision essentials**
> **Cash:** the money the firm holds in notes and coins and in its bank accounts.
> **Cash flow:** the movement of money into and out of the firm's bank account.

Exercises

(A and B: 20 marks; 25 minutes)

A Read the unit, then ask yourself:

1 Why do businesses think that money in bank accounts is part of their cash total? (2)
2 How might a house-building firm suffer if it lacks the cash to buy supplies of bricks in bulk? (4)
3 Outline two cash flow problems a British seaside hotel business might have. (4)
4 Before her first beauty salon opened, Moira Angell's builders took four months to complete the work – exactly double what they had promised. Outline two ways this would affect the cash position of the business. (4)

B Look at the cash flow table (below) for a one-year-old women's clothes shop.

Explain two ways in which the cash position of the business might be improved. (6)

Cash flow for a women's clothes shop

ALL FIGURES IN £000S	JANUARY	FEBRUARY	MARCH	APRIL
Cash at start of month	90	94	85	83
Cash in	24	16	18	22
Cash out	20	25	20	22
Net monthly cash flow	4	–9	–2	0
Cash at end of month	94	85	83	83

Unit 20 The role and importance of cash

Practice questions

(20 marks; 25 minutes)

Cash crisis at Bury

Cash is king in every business, but especially in professional sport. Before the start of every season supporters press their clubs to invest heavily to bring about success. Yet only a small number of clubs can succeed each year, so most will 'fail'.

In 2001 the failure of ITV Digital meant a drastic drop in TV income for all football clubs outside the Premiership. This had a huge impact on Bury FC, a small club that had rebuilt and modernised its ground to create a 12,000 all-seater stadium. In 2002 Bury FC put its entire playing staff up for sale in a desperate attempt to raise money. It did not help and the club went under.

Remarkably, hard work and fundraising by supporters enabled a fans' group to buy the club, helped hugely by the willingness of those owed money by Bury to accept being paid just 10p per pound of debt. The accountants who handled these arrangements said: 'Selling the club to its supporters enables the club to become an integral part of the local community. This solution could well provide the basis for other clubs to deal with the cash flow difficulties they are currently facing.'

Sadly, in 2005 the financial problems were no better, as falling attendance led to two winding-up orders being served on the club. Again the supporters worked miracles to try to raise more funds, helped by Manchester United's Gary Neville. The problem remains, however, with monthly interest charges of £10,000, on top of the operating losses from running a club with (in 2005) average attendances of just 2500.

With cash flow problems, prevention is much easier than cure.

Questions

1. What is meant by the term 'cash flow'? (2)
2. Identify and explain two reasons why Bury's cash position became so serious. (4)
3. a) What percentage of Bury's ground capacity is being used by its average crowd of 2500? (3)
   b) What cash problems might that lead to? (4)
4. Explain why, with cash flow problems, prevention is much easier than cure. (7)

21 Forecasting cash flow

Cash flow is the difference between the flows of cash into and out of a business over a period of time. For example, if a firm starts up by spending £20,000 of cash on premises and stock in its first month, but receives only £1000 from sales to customers, its month 1 cash flow is *minus* £19,000.

Cash flow forecasting means predicting the future flows of cash into and out of the firm's bank account. In effect, it means forecasting what the bank balance will look like at the end of each month. A cash flow forecast will usually be for a 12-month period. The table below, though, shows the forecast cash flow for the first six months of a brand new nightclub, started with £250,000 of capital. The forecast is based on some key points:

- Building work is finished by the end of September, so that customers can start coming in October.
- A launch party will bring the publicity and the customers needed for success.
- Costs will prove as expected, so the business never has to dip into the overdraft.

Forecast cash flow for new nightclub

(FIGURES IN £000s)	AUGUST	SEPTEMBER	OCTOBER	NOVEMBER	DECEMBER	JANUARY
Cash at start	250	65	10	20	25	55
Cash in	0	0	85	65	115	55
Cash out	185	55	75	60	85	60
Net monthly cash	(185)	(55)	10	5	30	(5)
Cash at month end	65	10	20	25	55	50

Successful cash flow forecasts require:

- accurate prediction of monthly sales revenues
- accurate prediction of when customers will pay for the goods they have bought
- careful allowance for operating costs and the timing of payments

- careful allowance for other flows of cash, such as cash outflows when purchasing assets such as land, and inflows from raising additional capital, perhaps from selling shares.

This level of accuracy is very hard to achieve, especially for new, small firms. This is a key reason why the failure rate is so high among new firms. If cash flow proves much worse than the forecast, banks can be unforgiving. If a firm enters a period of **negative cash flow** without having discussed it with the bank, the consequences can be serious. If a bank loses confidence in a client, it can demand to have the overdraft withdrawn within 24 hours. This is likely to make it impossible for the business to continue trading.

The importance of cash flow forecasts

Forecasting cash inflows and outflows is always important, especially for three types of business:

- new firms
- fast-growing firms
- firms with erratic sales (e.g. a firework factory that only really brings in cash in October and November – how will it pays its bills from January to August?).

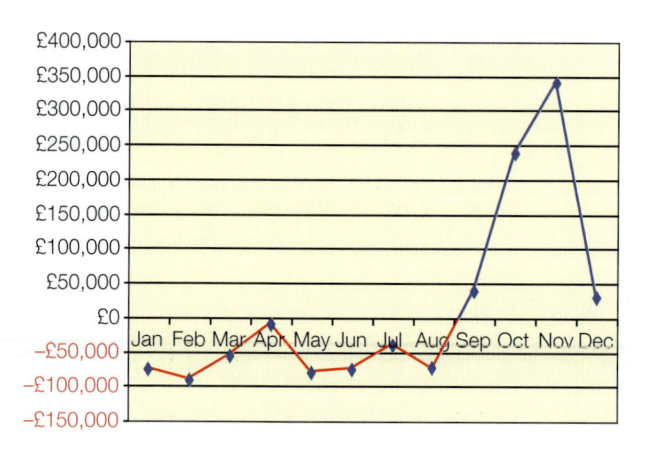

Monthly cash flow at a firework factory

Negative cash flow

When cash outflows are greater than inflows the result is negative cash flow. In other words, the firm is operating in the red. This is sustainable for a few weeks or months, as long as the firm has an overdraft facility or other sources of capital. Ideally, though, the business should act to improve its cash flow.

There are many ways a firm can act to improve its cash position.

1. **Cut stock levels** (i.e. reduce the money the business has tied up in stocks of goods it means to use or to sell). If a firm cancels or reduces its orders to suppliers, stocks will steadily fall and so too will the amount of cash tied up. A £40,000 reduction in the levels of stock being held will place £40,000 in the firm's bank account.
2. **Increase credit from suppliers** (i.e. take a longer period before paying the companies that have supplied you with goods). This delays your cash outflows, which will improve the cash flow.
3. **Reduce credit to customers**. By giving less time to pay, you are getting your cash more quickly. This may cause some problems if customers go to someone with longer credit terms. Overall, though, it may be better to deal with few, good payers than some who take ages to pay.

Conclusion

Careful cash flow forecasting is the single most important way to keep a bank manager's confidence. That, in turn, makes it easier and cheaper to borrow some extra cash when the business needs it. The word 'careful' implies cautious. In other words, the bank manager will be impressed if a business keeps its forecasts of cash inflow quite low; while expecting the worst of cash outflows. If the cash position always turns out a little better than expected, who could object?

Revision essentials
Cash flow forecasting: predicting the future flows of cash into and out of the firm's bank account.
Negative cash flow: when cash out is greater than cash in.
Net monthly cash: the month's cash inflow *minus* the month's cash outflow.

Exercises

(25 marks; 25 minutes)

Read the unit, then ask yourself:

1. Give two benefits of cash flow forecasting for a new, small firm. (2)
2. Look at the table on page 89, showing the forecast cash flow for a new nightclub.
   a) Explain briefly two reasons why the firm's cash has fallen from £250,000 at the start of August to £10,000 by the end of September. (4)
   b) Explain briefly the likely effect on the firm's cash position if the builders worked too slowly, forcing the nightclub to open in November rather than October. (4)
3. Look at the graph on page 90, showing monthly cash flow at a firework factory.
   a) Estimate each month's cash flow (read it off the graph), then add up the figures to estimate the firm's cash flow over the whole year. (5)
   b) Why might the firework company have faced serious financial problems by August? (5)
4. Explain in your own words why it is sensible to forecast cash flows cautiously. (5)

Practice questions (20 marks; 25 minutes)

THYME RUNS OUT

In April 2002 a famously mean restaurant critic wrote a glowing review of a new restaurant called Thyme, in Clapham, South London. He loved the cooking and the terrific value for money. By spring 2003 its two chefs were picking up an award for the Best New Restaurant in London. Thyme was packed every night and turning people away.

Frustrated by packing people into quite a small restaurant, the two chefs decided to look for bigger premises. In early 2004 they found a terrific space in Covent Garden, in central London. The rental payments on the lease were huge, so they decided to make the menu more expensive (one option was a 'tasting menu' at £100 per person!). For many months a huge sum was invested in creating a beautiful restaurant with the finest kitchen equipment and fittings, plus a huge wine cellar filled with expensive wines.

In November 2004 Thyme closed in Clapham and opened in Covent Garden. Initial restaurant reviews were positive about the quality of the food, but shocked at the prices. One reviewer noted that 'They have had the Thyme logo printed on the napkins and the knives. Clearly money has been no object.' He also noted that he and his wife were the only diners in the huge 86-seat restaurant. In July 2005 Thyme closed down. It had run out of cash.

Questions

1 Outline the likely cash flow position of the Clapham restaurant between mid-2002 and early 2004. (3)
2 Identify two causes of high cash outflows at the time of the move. (2)
3 Explain why a cash flow forecast would have been especially useful for Thyme during its expansion in 2004. (6)
4 Discuss the mistakes you believe Thyme's owners made that led to the July 2005 closure. (9)

22 Raising finance

In 2005 Martin Halstead, aged 19, started **AlphaOne Airways**. This airline was to fly between Oxford and Cambridge, though its focus switched to flying in and out of the Isle of Man. Martin financed the start-up in three ways:

- his own capital
- the capital of family and friends
- an investment by a friend based in the Middle East.

Martin's personal capital came from selling his first business – a software company that he had started at the age of 15.

Although Martin had more than £250,000 of **share capital** to start with, the costs of building an airline meant that he soon needed to look for more finance. This came partly from more share capital and partly from loans. Martin's goal in all negotiations about extra capital was to make sure he kept a 51 per cent stake in his business. He knew that owning a majority of the shares would keep him in charge.

When raising finance there are three vital questions to ask.

1. **How secure is the source?** Capital raised by selling shares is kept within the business permanently, which means it is 100 per cent secure. Bank overdrafts, by contrast, can be cancelled at any time, allowing the bank to demand its money back within 24 hours.
2. **How expensive is the source?** When starting a business, capital can be expensive to obtain, because investors want high rewards to balance against the risk of possibly losing the money they invest.
3. **Is enough being raised?** Because capital is hard to raise and expensive to manage, many firms raise just enough to cover their expected needs. Unfortunately, it is hard to anticipate all possible problems in starting up and running a business, so it is wise to obtain at least 25 per cent more finance than seems necessary. This provides a safety net.

Short-, medium- and long-term finance

When raising finance, the first question to ask is about the timing of the cash requirement. Is the finance needed for a few weeks or for several years? If a business wants to buy a 10-year lease on a shop, there is clearly a need for ten years of financing. Therefore it would be crazy to finance this via an overdraft, which is a useful, but expensive, way of borrowing money in the short term.

The rule is simple: short-term needs require short-term finance; long-term needs require long-term finance.

Long-term finance can be used to:

- provide start-up capital to finance the business for its whole life span
- finance the purchase of assets with a long life, such as property and buildings
- provide capital for expansion, such as building a new, bigger factory or buying up another business.

Medium-term finance can be used to:

- finance the purchase of assets with a two- to five-year life, such as cars, lorries and computer systems
- finance a change of business strategy, such as switching marketing focus from Britain to the whole of Europe
- replace an overdraft that is proving expensive.

Short-term finance can be used to:

- get through periods when cash flow is poor for seasonal reasons (e.g. a seaside hotel during the winter)
- bridge gaps when large customers delay payment, leaving no cash coming in to pay the bills
- provide the extra cash needed when a sudden, rush order requires a large sum to buy raw materials and pay overtime wages.

Types of long-term finance
Share capital

Ordinary shares give the buyer part-ownership of the business. If you buy 100 shares in a firm that has a total of 1000 shares, you own 10 per cent of the business. This gives you voting rights at the annual general meeting and entitles you to 10 per cent of any **dividends** paid from the firm's profits.

For the business, share capital has two key benefits.

1. The business has the capital permanently; if shareholders want to cash in their shares, they can only do so by finding someone else to buy them (usually through the stock market); they cannot get their money back from the company.

2. In a bad year no dividends need to be paid. Whereas interest payments to banks must be paid, no matter what, shareholders are not promised a dividend payment every year. So if the firm cannot afford to pay dividends, it need not do so; this makes share capital a safer source of finance than bank loans.

Drawbacks to businesses of share capital are:

- if lots of shares are issued, ownership gets spread thinly among many shareholders; this dilutes the power of the founders of the business. The key to retaining control is to keep hold of more than 50 per cent of the shares
- if the business is listed on the stock exchange it becomes vulnerable to takeover bids. This might affect decision making within the firm, for example forcing the whole business to be greedier for profit than would otherwise be the case (because high profits mean a high share price, making the business expensive to take over).

Loan capital

Loan capital is any source of borrowing, probably from a bank. It might be in the form of a mortgage for as long as 20 years, or a bank loan for 5–8 years. The key features of loan capital are that:

- interest payments must be paid on time or there is a risk of being taken to court and perhaps closed down
- almost all loans are secured against the assets the firm owns; therefore failure to pay means losing an asset, such as buildings, shops or lorries
- the interest charges may be fixed or variable; some firms like fixed rates (e.g. 7 per cent a year, fixed for the five-year life of the loan); others like variable rates.

Venture capital

This is a combination of share and loan capital. Providers of **venture capital** will take risks, as long as they can share in the rewards. Therefore they want a share stake in the business, though often offering a bank loan in addition. For a young or growing firm, a venture capital company is more likely to provide finance than a large high-street bank.

Profit

Over 60 per cent of all funds for business expansion come from the profits made by firms. This is the ideal source of capital, as it does not require the payment of interest charges or dividends. Well-run businesses fund as much of their capital needs as possible from the profits they make from their regular trading.

Entrepreneurs meeting venture capitalists

Types of medium-term finance

Loan capital

As for 'Types of long-term finance', above, but covering two- to five-year loans.

Leasing

This is a way of obtaining the use of important assets without ever buying them. Many company cars are leased. All this means is signing a contract committing the business to make regular payments on a car over a period that is usually two or three years.

Types of short-term finance

Bank overdraft

This is the most common form of finance. It must be understood in two parts. First, the bank grants the business (or individual) an overdraft facility, for example of £5000. This provides the right to keep spending until the bank account is £5000 in the red. The actual overdraft level is likely to vary day by day, and even hour by hour, as customers pay up or staff salaries are paid out.

Key features of a bank overdraft are:

- variable interest rate (i.e. the cost of borrowing money will rise if UK interest rates rise); this adds a degree of uncertainty to small business plans
- flexibility: instead of having a £5000 bank loan, requiring payments each month based on the whole sum, a £5000 overdraft facility need only be dipped into occasionally. So if a firm only needs to borrow money for one day, it will pay 1/365th of the annual interest rate
- the bank can demand full repayment of an overdraft within 24 hours. Many of the firms that go into **liquidation** have been finished off by banks that make this demand.

Trade credit

Small firms rely hugely upon good relationships with suppliers. Big companies can bully their way to get what they want from suppliers; small firms have to be nice or clever. If a supplier knows and trusts a customer, it may be willing to help when the customer is in need. For example, a small clothes shop may be able to persuade Stella McCartney to keep supplying clothes even though the shop has not yet paid earlier bills. Getting a longer credit period is an effective way to raise short-term finance.

For small business start-ups, though, it is often impossible to obtain credit at the start. Suppliers demand to be paid cash in advance or on delivery. After all, they do not know whether you will be among the 30 per cent of firms that fail to survive their first year.

Conclusion

When deciding how to raise capital, the starting point is to identify how much you need and how long you need it for. Broadly, there are three options.

1. Loan capital.
2. Share capital.
3. Internal sources, such as reinvesting the profit the firm is making.

Most experts would then advise balancing out the capital; in other words, not relying too much on share capital and/or loans.

> **Revision essentials**
> **Dividends:** payments to shareholders from the company's yearly profits. The directors of the company decide how large a dividend payment to make; in a bad year they can decide on zero.
> **Liquidation:** selling off a firm's assets in order to raise cash to pay off the firm's debts.
> **Share capital:** raising finance by selling part-ownership in the business. Shareholders have the right to question the directors and to receive part of the yearly profits.
> **Venture capital:** a combination of share capital and loan capital, provided by a bank that is willing to take a chance on the success of a small- to medium-sized business.

Exercises

(20 marks; 25 minutes)

Read the unit, then ask yourself:

1. Explain why the founder of a business is likely to care about keeping 51 per cent of the business's share capital. (4)
2. Identify whether the following situations require short-, medium- or long-term finance.
   a) Buying extra stock for the Christmas period. (1)
   b) Buying land nearby in case it is needed for expansion. (1)
   c) Redecorating your restaurant. (1)
   d) Buying a new company BMW for the managing director. (1)
3. Why is profit the ideal source of capital? (2)
4. Outline two possible advantages to an investor of buying shares in a business rather than lending it money. (4)
5. Explain why a fast-growing business might choose to obtain assets by leasing rather than buying them for cash. (3)
6. Explain the difference between an overdraft and an overdraft facility. (3)

Practice questions

(25 marks; 30 minutes)

In late 2004 young mum Leila Wilcox (24) and established businessman and mentor to entrepreneurs Ivan Massow started up a business called Halos n Horns. Leila invested £15,000, largely borrowed from her family, and Ivan put in a further £30,000. The business idea was a range of affordable, fun children's shampoos that are kind to the skin. They managed to find a manufacturer who could produce the right products. Their eventual product line-up was:

- Kids Berry Burst – shampoo and detangler;
- Kids Zingy Orange – hair and body wash;
- Kids Mango Melon Mayhem – shampoo and conditioner;
- Halo Baby Bath – kind to eyes.

Halos n Horns launched mid-2005 into Tesco, Somerfield, Sainsbury's and Ocado, resulting in an initial order of 200,000 bottles. This required £40,000 of capital to pay the manufacturer, before the bottles could be delivered to Tesco. The business can (just) afford this, but when sales take off, Tesco requires a further huge order that makes extra finance necessary. The team tries to sell more shares for £125,000, but eventually borrows the money needed.

With just 15p of profit per bottle, the business requires at least 500,000 sales to cover its yearly fixed costs. In fact, by the end of its first year Halos n Horns has made a profit of £61,000. With many other supermarkets queuing up to buy its children's shampoos, the business looks to have succeeded.

Questions

1. Outline one possible reason why the two founders only used share capital to finance the start-up of Halos n Horns. (4)
2. The manufacturer who produced the shampoos required to be paid in advance. Explain why it may not have been willing to give Halos n Horns any trade credit. (3)
3. a) Given the information about the manufacturing costs of producing 200,000 bottles, what is the apparent production price per bottle? (3)
   b) Given the 15p profit claimed per bottle, what appears to be Halos n Horns' selling price to Tesco? (2)
4. When further finance was needed, the team decided to borrow the extra money rather than sell more shares.
   a) Outline two possible reasons why the team may have decided against selling more shares in these circumstances. (4)
   b) Discuss whether an overdraft or a bank loan was the more appropriate way for Halos n Horns to borrow money. (9)

23 Objectives when starting up

People starting a new enterprise usually have one of three objectives.

1. A financial objective, such as to be rich.
2. A business **mission**, such as James Dyson in setting up his own bagless cleaner business; he was determined to prove that his idea would work.
3. A social mission, such as starting a charity aimed at improving water quality in African villages.

Financial objectives

When starting up, most entrepreneurs concentrate on survival. In other words, they want to bring in enough cash to pay the bills. They will only think about profit when the business is doing well enough to mean some cash is building up in the bank account. From then on, the owner can make decisions based on profit and therefore wealth. Innocent Drinks, founded in 1998, was estimated to be worth £100 million to Pepsi or Coca-Cola within eight years. It had always been profitable, but the key to its huge value was that both the American drinks giants could see huge potential from joining Innocent's quirky image to their own distribution muscle.

If a business is being set up with a view to making the owners rich, there are some key points to bear in mind:

- the product or service must have high value added (i.e. customers must be willing to pay a high price for something that does not cost much to make or provide); the Pizza Express chain is worth more than £400 million, and the value has come from the high prices that can be charged for tomato paste smeared on bread, which is what the average pizza really is
- it must be possible for the product or service to be provided and sold to a large market, perhaps using mass production or a sales system such as franchising; this allows the good idea to be reproduced many times over

- it must be possible to protect the idea from being copied by others. James Dyson took out **patents** to protect his new cleaner (and sued Hoover successfully).

Business mission

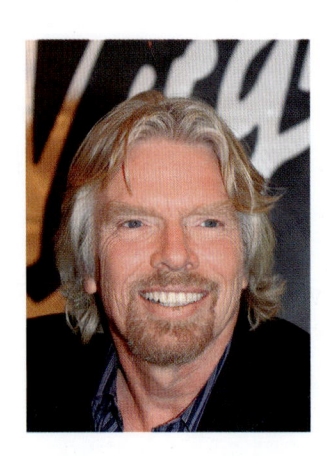

Many people start a business from a sense of purpose, even duty. They think they can do something better than anyone else. In 2005 the American Glazer family bought up Manchester United. Angry fans responded by setting up 'FC United' as their own team. The original **Body Shop** was started in Brighton because Anita Roddick could not find the type of cosmetics she wanted to use herself. Business ideas such as these may start up with no desire for profit other than to help finance survival and growth. Later, the owners may realise there is money to be made. Anita Roddick has become very wealthy from Body Shop (over £30 million), even though it was not her original goal.

There are other sources of business mission. It may be that the individual is determined to start a business for personal reasons, such as to prove him or herself. A surprising number of successful entrepreneurs are dyslexic (dyslexia is word-blindness, making it difficult to read and write), for example Richard Branson and Anita Roddick. Their feelings of failure at school are said to have motivated them to build dynamic business empires.

There are also many people who start a business because they want to be their own boss. They want to have more control over their working life than is possible when you work for someone else. John Cauldwell (billionaire boss of **Phones4U**) started work as a tyre fitter at a Michelin factory. His objective when he started his first business was to bring his life under his own control.

Social mission

The not-for-profit sector is becoming increasingly important. This refers to enterprises that are started with the objective of achieving a social goal, using business methods. A traditional example is a charity such as **Oxfam**, which is professionally run, but has the goal of helping to relieve suffering in developing countries. Today, firms such as **One** (not-for-profit bottled water) attempt to achieve the same objectives, but not necessarily as a charity (because charity status requires a great deal of paperwork).

A leading social enterprise is **Traidcraft**, which began in 1979 and has built up its turnover to £15 million a year. All profits are ploughed back into the business. Traidcraft began the idea of 'trade not aid' by bringing coffee, tea and household items from developing countries and selling them in the UK. It helped to found the hugely successful **Cafédirect** and **Fairtrade** businesses. Both specialise in offering developing-country producers guaranteed higher prices for their output, and then finding sales outlets in Britain. The founder of Traidcraft, Richard Adams, earns a salary from running the organisation, but his enterprising approach has never been in the pursuit of profit.

Other firms with social rather than profit motives include:

- the Co-op Bank, which is owned by its members
- Waitrose and John Lewis, which are owned by their staff
- groups such as Greenpeace and Friends of the Earth.

Conclusion

It is a mistake to think that business is just about making profits. People run businesses because they can be challenging, rewarding and fun. They also provide the scope to achieve social as well as financial progress. Nevertheless, there will always be some firms that are interested only in profit. These may become the cowboy builders who charge high prices for shoddy jobs; or the financial institutions who encourage young people to build up debts they cannot afford. Just as every individual is different, so is every business.

Revision essentials
Mission: something that a person passionately wants to achieve.
Patent: legal protection for the originator of a technical breakthrough.

Exercises

(15 marks; 15 minutes)

Read the unit, then ask yourself:

1 Why should someone starting a business for financial objectives make sure to identify a product or service with high value added? (2)
2 Give two reasons why an entrepreneur might be justified in trying to make as much profit as possible from his/her new business. (2)
3 Which of the following motives might influence you to start a business of your own?
   a) To be your own boss.
   b) To prove yourself.
   c) To get rich.
   Pick one and explain why it matters most to you. (5)
4 Salvatore Falcone started his Italian bakery to have a business that could support his young family, then provide jobs for them when they grew up. Discuss whether his objectives could best be described as financial, business or social, or whether it is more of a mixture of the three. (6)

Practice questions

(20 marks; 25 minutes)

Organic enterprise

The Soil Association was started up in 1946 by a group of farmers and nutritionists. Set up as a charity, its purpose was to campaign against the use of chemicals in farming. No one listened for many years, making it hard for the charity to keep going on the limited contributions given by members. Then, in the 1990s, people started to get interested in organic farming. Problems such as mad cow disease made shoppers more careful about the food they ate.

As interest rose in organic farming, the Soil Association's charity status ensured that people trusted it to certify which products are truly organic and which are not. Now, in 2005, UK sales of organic foods are more than £1200 million, and rising by 10 per cent a year. The Association is at the heart of this, with 140 staff supervising the approval of most of the organic food sold in the UK. Having started as a small-scale social enterprise, the Association has become quite a powerful organisation. It remains a charity, however, run for and by its members.

Questions

1 a) Explain the objectives of those who set up the Soil Association. (4)
  b) At the start of the chapter, three types of business objective were identified. Into which of the three categories would you place this case? (1)
2 Explain why it might be important for a charity such as the Soil Association to control its costs as carefully as any business. (6)
3 Discuss why the Association's charity status ensured that people were more trusting of it than they might have been with an ordinary company. (9)

SECTION 4

MAKING THE START-UP EFFECTIVE

24 Introduction to effective start-up

In July 2000 Steve and Julie Pankhurst opened a website called **Friends Reunited**. It was to enable old school friends to get back in contact. It was completely free to register and use the site.

As they had no money for marketing the site, all their resources went into making the site as user-friendly as possible. By the end of 2000 they only had 3000 registered members, and just a tiny income from advertising. Early in 2001 the site was featured on a Radio 2 show, and tens of thousands tried to register. The computer system collapsed, but was put right overnight, and by February there were 19,000 members. With rising costs (they built up from a single computer server in January to 15 by the summer), they introduced a £5 charge for making contact with friends. This was well timed, as **word of mouth** enabled membership to shoot ahead to 1 million by August. By the end of 2001 it had risen to 4 million.

Friends Reunited continued to grow and develop until, in December 2005, ITV bought the site for £120 million, with a further £55 million to be paid in 2009, if profit targets are met. Steve and Julie are believed to get a quarter of this cash.

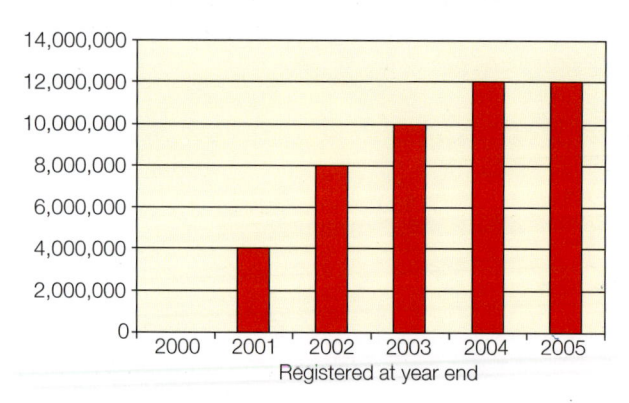

Friends Reunited registered users

Making a start-up work

The keys to the success of Friends Reunited provide a model for every new business.

1. **Customer focus.** Julie and Steve believed in their **vision**: bringing people together. They encouraged people to write emails about how their reunions had gone, and tried to answer every one. They cherished stories like the first Friends Reunited engagement, then

marriage, then – in August 2002 – baby. In response to customer feedback and ideas, they introduced Genes Reunited, to allow people to check their family tree, and bring together people who did not know they were related.

2 **Effective delivery.** The site has always done 'what it says on the tin'. Some businesses promise a great deal, but struggle to get the details right. This leaves the customer frustrated or even bitter. Friends Reunited does not charge for looking for an old friend. You only pay when you have found someone – and want to make contact.

3 **Intelligent business organisation and financing.** In its early stages, Friends Reunited became a **limited liability** business. This ensured that any serious financial problems for the business would not create personal liabilities for Julie and Steve. It also made it easier to bring in new investors to become shareholders in the business. This was essential, as the business was swallowing cash at an alarming rate in 2001. By the time of the 2005 sale, the Pankhursts owned just 25 per cent of the shares – but they were worth more than £30 million!

4 **Great management of people.** To cope with 2001's growth of over 1300 per cent (from 3000 to 4 million) was an astonishing achievement. It required rapid recruitment and training of new staff, all of whom worked from home until an office was opened in 2002. Julie Pankhurst, when interviewed in late 2001, said that she delegated a great deal to her 15 staff. In other words, she trusted staff to get on with things without checking up on them all the time. This is a great way to motivate employees, as long as they feel free to ask for help when needed.

Other factors in start-up success are:

- **Luck.** The best ideas can be undermined by bad luck, such as the launch of a holiday company focusing on the American South, two months before New Orleans was devastated by hurricane. In the case of Friends Reunited, the Radio 2 show came at the right time to push the business forward. Without it, Steve and Julie might have lost heart and given up.
- **Flexibility.** A business needs to be based on a clear idea, but the managers must be willing to change in line with experience. Friends Reunited was meant to be a totally free site, with income coming solely from advertising. The decision to start charging in early 2001 was crucial to provide the revenue to cover the costs of expansion.
- **Hard work.** The golfer Arnold Palmer once said, 'It's a funny thing, the more I practise the luckier I get.' In other words, hard work pays off. Julie and Steve had to work extremely hard during 2000 and 2003, both to keep everything working day by day, and to find the time to think ahead about new products and new ideas. The 2005 cheque for £30 million will have eased the pain!

SECTION 4 Making the start-up effective

> **Revision essentials**
> **Limited liability:** where responsibility for paying the debts of the business is limited to the business, and cannot be passed on to the owners (the shareholders).
> **Vision:** a clear view of what the business should be aiming for (e.g. bringing millions of people together).
> **Word of mouth:** people speaking to each other about a topic or a business.

Exercises
(25 marks; 30 minutes)

Read the unit, then ask yourself:

1 Explain one reason why businesses should take word of mouth very seriously. (3)
2 Explain the importance of customer focus in running one of the following businesses:
   a) Manchester United FC
   b) Primark
   c) McDonald's. (4)
3 How might effective delivery affect word of mouth? (4)
4 Outline two possible benefits to a business of having well-motivated staff. (4)
5 a) Outline two occasions where luck played a factor in Steve and Julie's success. (4)
   b) Discuss whether luck was the most important reason for Steve and Julie's success. (6)

Practice questions
(20 marks; 25 minutes)

Having competed for three years at the White Air extreme sports festival on the Isle of Wight, Damon Breeze decided to start his own sports business. As one of the world's top kitesurfers, he was sure that his name would be a good basis for a website selling extreme sports clothing and equipment, from kitesurfing and mountaineering through to snowboarding and mountain-boarding.

He took advice from a business-minded aunt, then formed a limited company called Extreme

Breeze Ltd. His aunt invested £18,000 and received 49 per cent of the shares. She urged him to keep focused on selling to the core market of young, male, extreme sports fans.

Damon had always been good with computers, but hired a specialist to build the site. It took three months and cost £14,000. It opened on 1 July 2005 and immediately made a sale. Because the business was so short of cash, it hadn't bought any stock, so relied on buying from suppliers and delivering to customers as quickly as possible. Several complaints came Damon's way, when deliveries were much slower than promised.

By October, enough cash had come in to start buying items for stock. This made it possible to deliver within the five days customers were promised. Even so, progress was quite slow. Damon was hoping to make sizeable profits within a few months of starting up the business. It was not going to be that easy.

Questions

1. Outline two weaknesses in Damon's business start-up. (4)
2. a) What is meant by a 'limited company'? (3)
   b) Explain why it was wise to set up a limited company in this case. (4)
3. Why is it usually very difficult to make sizeable profits within a few months of starting up a business? (4)
4. If you were invited to invest at this stage, what changes would you insist on beforehand? Explain your reasoning. (5)

25 Customer focus and the marketing mix

Every year Britain's business leaders are asked to vote for their 'Most Admired' business boss. For three years in a row they have voted for Terry Leahy, chief executive of **Tesco**. In a magazine interview, Leahy gave his 'Secrets for Success' as follows:

- Have a clear vision.
- Listen to your customers.
- Trust your staff to make decisions.
- Keep things simple.

This unit is about listening to your customers.

Customer focus

If you run a small, one-person business, **customer focus** comes from chatting to and learning from customers, face-to-face. This is much harder for Terry Leahy, as Tesco has tens of millions of customers. His solution is to leave his office every Friday and visit stores, staff and shoppers. This is time-consuming, but invaluable. He learns when shoppers are unhappy with the products or the service. Indeed he insists that every director and thousands of head office managers spend one week a year back in a store, stacking shelves and working at the tills. This keeps everyone focused on the key to the business – customer satisfaction.

Customer focus can enable a business to learn:

- about niggles/weaknesses
- how customers see you in relation to your competitors
- what else customers want (this might lead to new products or services)
- what customers do not want, or what they would quite like to have, but not enough to pay for it.

A mystery shopper can test the standard of customer service

There are a number of different ways to achieve customer focus.

1. Train staff to be clear that customers are the purpose (and the paymaster) of the business. Ideally every employee should test everything they do by asking: how does this benefit the customer? The reason many people love the chefs Jamie Oliver and Gordon Ramsay is because this attitude shines through. Both show incredible determination to do their best, all the time.
2. Check regularly on customer views (e.g. by market research). This should investigate consumers' attitudes to different products and brands, their buying habits and their views on new product ideas.
3. Get senior managers to act as 'mystery shoppers' (i.e. acting as an ordinary customer to find out what happens when you shop at the Newcastle branch or phone with a query).
4. Ensure that targets set for staff are focused on customer satisfaction and not on short-term sales. On many occasions UK banks have been guilty of persuading customers to buy inappropriate financial products. Sales staff greedily pursued commission based on short-term sales – and sometimes cost customers thousands of pounds. Examples include endowment mortgages, personal pensions and 'precipice' bonds. Not only are such actions **unethical**, but they also damage the reputation of the business.

Marketing mix

It may not be enough to have a clear customer focus and to rely on word of mouth. If a market is already crowded with lots of brands, it may be impossible to get established without a heavy marketing campaign. Success will hinge on the marketing mix chosen by the company.

The marketing mix is the way in which a firm tries to ensure that the right product is being promoted in the right way and sold at the right price at the right place. The mix is often called the four Ps:

- Product
- Price
- Promotion
- Place.

Unit 25 *Customer focus and the marketing mix*

> *'Marketing is the whole business seen from the customer's point of view.'*
> Peter Drucker, management guru

Product

After careful market research, a firm should be able to design a product or service that will appeal to a specific **target audience**. This is the heart of the mix, and the other three factors should revolve around this. For example, **Kellogg's** Special K cereal has always been targeted at weightwatchers. Having the right product to appeal to the audience is then backed up by:

- the 'right' price – more expensive than other cereals, to help confirm that it is worth paying for
- the right place – distributed in supermarkets and grocers, but also sold at breakfast bars in health clubs
- the right promotion – focusing the TV advertising at women, with a voice-over emphasising health (the 2005 'drop a jean size' campaign helped sales rise by 33 per cent).

Price

All consumers expect value for money; this means that price is always important. In many cases, having a low price may be crucial to achieving high sales, for instance when selling packets of sugar or butter. At other times, though, being 'cheap' may cause image problems. No one wants cheap baby food or cut-price perfume.

Most products are price-makers or price-takers. A price-maker has the market power to set prices that others have to follow. This can be true of new products (such as the **Innocent Drinks** smoothie, priced at an amazing £2 for a small bottle) or of established ones (such as **Chanel Nº5** perfume – £75 for a remarkably small bottle). Consumers see both these products as unique, and therefore are willing to pay a high price.

A price-taker is a product or service that has to be priced with reference to others in the marketplace. Perhaps it needs to be priced below the price leader (e.g. Tesco baked beans compared with **Heinz**); or perhaps the whole market is full of similar products (e.g. **Esso** petrol compared with **BP** or **Shell**).

Promotion

> *'Build a better mousetrap and the world will beat a path to your door.'*
> R. W. Emerson, management thinker

This is the way a firm can promote sales of its products. It lumps together methods of promoting the long-term image and sales of the business, using methods such as TV or cinema advertising, and short-term methods such as sales promotions (e.g. buy one get one free).

Most large firms are keen to use every £ spent on advertising to promote the long-term image of the product. Short-term boosts to sales can be at the expense of the brand image. Few firms would want to take such a risk.

Place

This is where (and how) the product is distributed, so that customers can get it when they want it. Mass market products usually seek as much distribution as possible. **Coca-Cola** uses the phrase 'an arm's length from desire'; in other words, they want such good distribution that customers should only need to stretch out an arm to get a Coke. Coca-Cola wants this (which is why there are so many vending machines) because they know that the more people see Coke, the more they buy.

For other products, the same does not apply. Chanel hates cut-price retailers such as **Superdrug** selling its perfumes; its managers worry that cutting prices may damage the image of the brand.

Examples of marketing mix in action

	CADBURY DAIRY MILK	**STARBUCKS**
Product	Traditional-tasting chocolate aimed at a mass market (i.e. 'everyone loves…').	Huge variety of coffees and other drinks; terrific space for sitting and relaxing.
Price	Priced competitively, to get high sales in the mass market.	Priced very high to fit in with the image of self-indulgence.
Promotion	Uses TV advertising and extensive promotional support (e.g. 25% extra chocolate at the same price).	Very little advertising; relies on location and word of mouth.
Place	Widespread distribution through sweetshops, grocers and other outlets.	Locations are clustered, effectively swamping an area with Starbucks.

Successful marketing mix

For success, a firm must make sure that its mix is coordinated and coherent. A classy product aimed at a classy market should have a high price, be promoted in classy magazines and stocked at the classiest shops. Similarly, a product aimed at the environmentally conscious buyer should have little advertising support, a moderate price premium and aim to be sold through a limited number of local outlets. The marketing mix puts the public face on a product or service. That face must make sense.

Revision essentials

Customer focus: keeping your staff thinking about customers' needs and wants.
Target audience: the part of the market your product is aimed at (e.g. women aged 15–24).
Unethical: doing something that is morally wrong (e.g. selling cigarettes to children you know are under 14 years).

Exercises

(20 marks; 25 minutes)

Read the unit, then ask yourself:

1 Why may customer focus be easier in a small business than in a big one? (3)
2 Outline two possible benefits to Tesco from getting all their directors to spend one week a year as shop-floor employees. (4)

3 Outline the marketing mix used by one of the following:
   a) Cadbury Creme Egg
   b) Tesco stores
   c) Ryanair. (5)
4 Why would 'buy one get one free' be a poor way to boost the long-term image and sales of a business? (4)
5 Explain one reason why Chanel may be right, and one reason why it might be wrong, in trying to stop Superdrug from stocking Chanel N°5 perfume. (4)

Practice questions (30 marks; 30 minutes)

In early 2005 Twinings launched an 'Everyday Tea'. Before then, Twinings had only focused on special teas such as Earl Grey. Now it was going head-to-head with the big beasts, Tetley and PG Tips.

Twinings' marketing idea was to launch a tea with a comparable taste to Tetley and PG, but with a superior image, backed by the 300-year-old Twinings brand. TV commercials featured the actor Stephen Fry, known for his good taste and his Englishness. Twinings Everyday Tea would sell at a 20 per cent price premium to Tetley and PG. The new product would be promoted by £4.5 million spent on TV and radio advertising. The distribution would be through supermarkets and grocers, plus restaurants and hotels.

The effectiveness of Twinings' marketing mix can be seen in the figures below.

Twinings' UK annual retail sales, 2004 and 2005

	2004	2005
Tetley	£132.3m	£130.1m
PG Tips	£129.7m	£123.9m
Twinings	£49.8m	£56.3m

(Source: A. C. Nielsen quoted in *The Grocer*, 17 December 2005)

Questions

1 Outline the marketing mix used by Twinings to launch its new Everyday Tea. (8)
2 a) Outline two actions the managers of PG Tips might have taken at the time of the Everyday Tea launch. (4)
   b) Briefly explain the reason for taking those actions. (4)
3 a) Calculate the percentage sales change between 2004 and 2005 for each of the three tea brands. (6)
   b) To what extent does this provide proof of the success of Twinings' launch of its Everyday Tea? (8)

26 Is the customer always right?

The American department store owner Marshall Field once said, 'Right or wrong, the customer is always right.' This has become a common phrase among shopkeepers throughout the world. But is it right?

A survey by the retail recruitment firm Retailchoice.com, showed that 95 per cent of shopworkers say they face rude customers on a regular basis. One in five say they have been reduced to tears by customers. In such cases, the customer is not right. Store managers have a duty to protect their staff from serious abuse. It is known as a **duty of care**. Typical examples would be the risks for railway staff or bus crews from drunk passengers late at night. The duty of management is to ensure that staff feel protected when dealing with difficult situations.

Even though it may be right to ban a customer, or even to call the police, the business should still try to learn from the incident. After all, the customer may have become frustrated by poor service. This might be the fault of the individual staff member or of the system as a whole. A passenger on a much-delayed train may be abusive to the guard, even though the problem is clearly not due to his/her negligence.

Other reasons the customer may not be right are:

- A customer may make life unpleasant for other customers, such as a noisy party held in a hotel room. There have been several incidents where airlines have had to restrain passengers who have been drunk and have abused other passengers, as well as airline staff.
- A customer may want to buy a house/car/phone that is glitzy, but not suitable. A good salesperson will try his/her best to persuade the customer to switch to a better option, but may have to accept defeat. A salesperson in a clothes shop honest enough to tell a customer not to buy an ill-fitting dress may ensure that the customer always comes back in future.
- No one has the right to insult another person. Some restaurant customers treat the waiters like servants. They have no right to do so. Employees deserve respect.

In some cases, staff may face difficult situations on their own. If managers fail to show a duty of care, there are two possible approaches staff can take.

1. Join a **trade union**. Unions act on behalf of staff at work, and would be quick to insist that managers show the responsibility that the law says they should show.
2. Write to the Health and Safety Executive (HSE) and insist on seeing a health and safety inspector; the Health and Safety at Work Act provides protection for those at work.

When starting up

When starting a small business, it is understandable to treat every customer with kid gloves. Yet there are some crucial issues to consider.

- Customers who do not pay on time are a menace; they disrupt your cash flow and there may be a risk that they will not pay at all; if necessary, a firm must be willing to ask a bad payer to pay in cash or go elsewhere.
- Customers may be so pushy about discounts that their business is not worth having. If a small firm is dealing with Tesco, it may be impossible to get a profitable price; if necessary, the firm should refuse to supply.

Despite these big reservations, when building a small business the owner may decide to put up with difficult, even unprofitable, customers. As long as there is a plan for changing things later on, this may not be a bad idea

Revision essentials
Duty of care: the employer's responsibilities to staff, which include assessing the physical risks and mental stresses of the job.
Trade union: a membership organisation for employees that provides protection and legal advice for issues that arise at work.

Exercises

(15 marks; 20 minutes)

Read the unit, then ask yourself:

1. Is the customer always right? (4)
2. Should a firm be willing to turn away profitable business from unpleasant customers? (4)
3. Outline two ways in which managers can train staff to cope better with difficult customers. (4)
4. Explain why cash flow is disrupted if customers fail to pay on time. (3)

Practice questions (15 marks; 15 minutes)

Unit 26 Is the customer always right?

Based in Wales, Walkers TV, Radio and Music Centre Ltd is a small electrical retail company with 3 shops and 11 staff. Most employees work at the shop counters and also deliver electrical goods or service them at customers' homes. All staff will, at some point, spend time working alone.

The shop's owners have developed a detailed programme for looking after their staff. This came about from incidents such as:

- verbal abuse on the telephone when a customer's television broke down three times
- a customer reacting angrily and becoming verbally abusive when a delivery was 20 minutes late
- activation of the panic alarm because of a drunk and disorderly customer in the shop.

The programme has included staff training focused on dealing with difficult customers. Often people are in a bad mood for an unrelated reason, so the key thing is to be calm and patient. The owners have also installed security systems such as CCTV and personal alarms for staff.

They believe that the benefits far outweigh the costs:

The benefits
- Staff are more confident to ask for assistance if they feel the need.
- Staff feel more secure and able to take on more work responsibilities.
- Staff know they have the support of their manager if any violence occurs.
- Staff are happy to do their jobs and do not avoid certain tasks because of the risks of violence – so more jobs get done.
- Dealing tactfully with customers results in improved customer satisfaction and reduced frustration. This leads to quick and effective service for customers.

The costs
- All measures to reduce violence are an accepted cost.
- Panic alarms may be expensive, but they can be made simply and cheaply using a large doorbell, light switch and battery (costs £5 to £10).
- Some measures are cost-effective because they have more than one purpose, for example CCTV doubles as a crime- and theft- prevention measure.

(Source: www.hse.gov.uk Crown copyright material is reproduced with the permission of the Controller of HMSO)

Questions

1. Identify two examples of management at Walkers showing a duty of care towards its staff. (2)
2. Explain how staff might feel about the level of support given to them by the management of Walkers electrical shop. (4)
3. Identify two ways in which Walkers' profit could be helped by its policy towards customers and its staff. (4)
4. Discuss what an employee might do if there were problems with customers, but no help available from managers. (5)

27 Limited versus unlimited liability

As many as half of all new businesses close down within three years. Each year over 12,000 companies go into liquidation (selling off the assets to pay off the debts), and in 2005 over 40,000 individuals were declared **bankrupt**. All business failures are painful, but there is a big difference between a company going into liquidation and an individual being made bankrupt.

When a company goes under, a **liquidator** is appointed to try to raise as much cash as possible to repay the firm's debts. If there is a shortfall, the company's owners (the shareholders) do not have to repay the debts. The losses of the shareholders are restricted to the money they invested in the business. This is known as **limited liability**. By investing in shares, they took a risk; but their gamble can only cost them the amount they invested, not a penny more. Their liability is limited.

By contrast, if the business had **unlimited liability**, financial disaster for the business will become a financial disaster for the owner or owners. Unpaid business debts could lead to the owner(s) losing their house, car and other possessions as part of bankruptcy proceedings. Yet this situation is completely unnecessary, as long as a business is run as a limited company.

Limited liability

To achieve limited liability, a business must be started up as a company. This requires an application to Companies House and the payment of around £150. Once the right forms have been filled in the business becomes a company. Small limited companies must put the letters 'Ltd' at the end of the company name. Large limited companies use the letters 'plc'.

The fee of £150 is a small sum to pay for improved financial security of the entrepreneur. There are also various other benefits from becoming a limited company.

- A company has share capital (perhaps 100 £1 shares), which makes it easy to divide up the ownership between different investors. As

long as the company's founder keeps hold of 51 per cent of the shares, s/he still has total control.
- If the business needs to raise more capital, it is quite easy to issue more shares for sale to other investors.
- The business continues to exist even if the founder of the business dies. The company develops a life of its own.
- Due to limited liability, the owners/shareholders can be bold about investing in the future of the business. If a bold move goes wrong, the business may suffer, but individual shareholders are not liable for the debts.

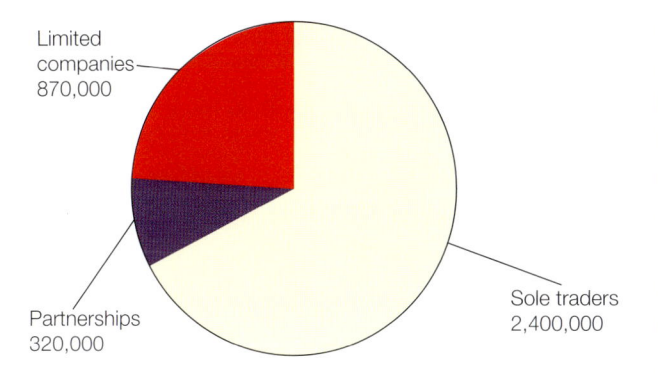

Given the advantages of limited liability, it is amazing that most businesses in the UK do not bother to turn into limited companies. Presumably the owners believe either that nothing can possibly go wrong, or that they will be able to cope financially even if something does go wrong. The clearest reason to avoid limited liability is that companies need to have their accounts drawn up by a qualified accountant. This means an annual cost of perhaps £1500 to be paid to an accountant.

Limited companies 870,000
Partnerships 320,000
Sole traders 2,400,000

Number of businesses in England and Wales, 2005

Unlimited liability

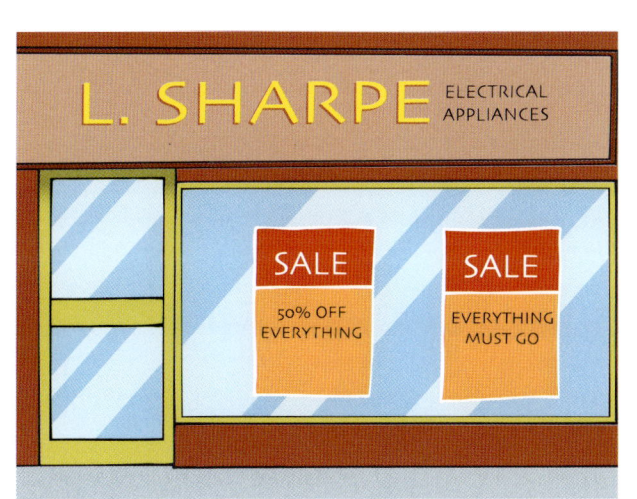

Anybody can start a business this afternoon. All that is needed is to tell HM Revenue and Customs and the National Insurance office. In few countries of the world is it so easy to start up. You would probably need a bank account, but is unlikely to be a problem unless you are trying to borrow large sums from the bank.

However, this business is not a limited company, and is therefore treated in the same way as the individual's own earnings. The business and the person are one and the same for tax and legal purposes. This is why failure by the business leaves the entrepreneur liable in full for any debts.

A person running her/his own business without forming a company is called a sole trader. It is also possible to join with others in a partnership. Sole traders and partnerships both have unlimited liability.

The only logical reason for ignoring limited liability (forming a company) is if there is no realistic possibility of debts building up. For example, if the business is a market stall, and goods are bought for cash in the morning and sold out by the afternoon, it is hard to see how debts could be built up. So why bother with the cost and paperwork involved in setting up a limited company?

Conclusion

Everyone starting a business should think seriously about forming a company and therefore having limited liability. This is especially important if money is being borrowed to finance the business. Individuals with unlimited liability should not take risks with borrowing or with credit.

> **Revision essentials**
>
> **Bankrupt:** An individual who is unable to pay his/her debts, even after all personal assets have been sold for cash.
>
> **Limited liability:** restricting the losses suffered by owners/shareholders to the sum they invested in the business.
>
> **Liquidator:** the person appointed to sell off a firm's assets and use the cash to repay as much as possible of the firm's debts.
>
> **Unlimited liability:** treating the business and the individual owner as inseparable, therefore making the individual responsible for all the debts of a failed business.

Exercises

(25 marks; 30 minutes)

Read the unit, then ask yourself:

1. Explain in your own words:
   a) limited liability (3)
   b) bankrupt. (3)
2. Why might an entrepreneur be reluctant to sell more than 50 per cent of the shares in his/her business? (3)
3. a) Use the figure on page 117 (Number of businesses in England and Wales) to calculate the percentage of businesses in England and Wales that have unlimited liability. (3)
   b) Outline one reason why businesses avoid becoming companies and therefore having limited liability. (2)
4. Explain why it is easier to make bold business decisions if your business is a limited company than if it is a sole trader with unlimited liability. (5)
5. K. V. Builders and Sons is an unlimited liability business that builds houses. It employs five people and borrows up to £150,000 to finance each job. Explain two reasons why it should form a company and therefore provide limited liability to its owners. (6)

Practice questions (20 marks; 20 minutes)

In recent years there has been an increase in the number of people becoming bankrupt. Some get into this state due to overspending on their credit cards, but more than half become bankrupt as a result of a business failure.

The most likely explanation for the increase is the high level of consumer debt. It is also possible that small, unlimited liability businesses are finding it harder to compete with big companies such as Tesco and Primark.

Whichever answer is the right one, the graph gives a clear signal to people starting up a business for the first time: form a limited company.

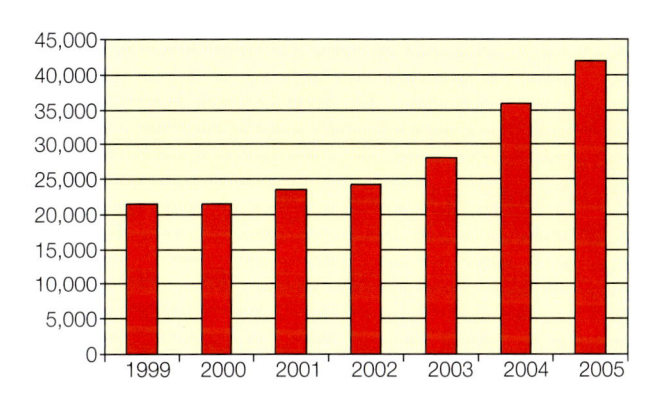

Bankruptcy orders in England and Wales, 1999–2005

Questions

1. What has been the approximate increase in bankruptcies between 1999 and 2005? (3)
2. Outline two reasons why a business might end up being unable to continue financially. (4)
3. The biggest category of bankrupt businesses is in the construction sector. Identify and explain two possible reasons why the building trade might have a high rate of business failure. (6)
4. Explain why the graph gives a clear signal to people setting up a business for the first time to form a limited company. (7)

28 Start-up legal and tax issues

In September 2000 Tamara Girvan opened a hairdresser's in Birmingham. It specialised in Afro-Caribbean hairstyles, and pitched itself as a smart, quite expensive, outlet. It did fantastically well, enabling Tamara to employ three trusted friends and four professional stylists. In 2003 a second shop was opened in the city centre, and it did even better. By 2005 Tamara employed 15 people and had a wage bill of over £180,000 a year. Her 2005 profits were over £85,000.

In mid-2005, however, Inland Revenue started an investigation into her personal tax position. The business had always been run as a sole trader, so the income of the business was the same as Tamara's personal income. The tax inspectors found that Tamara's record-keeping had not been great. Many of the items she claimed as costs had no paperwork/evidence to back them up. For example, in the early days she had paid a friend £500 in cash to install the plumbing. She had no record of this, therefore the tax inspectors refused to accept it as a business cost.

Eventually, with the help of an accountant, Tamara sorted out her tax problems. It cost her £18,000 plus £2200 in fines and £2500 to the accountant! Although the success of the business meant she could afford to pay, she always tells potential entrepreneurs to be very careful with the taxman.

The basics

When starting a business, the first rules are to tell HM Revenue and Customs (the taxman) and the **National Insurance** office. After that, just make sure to keep clear accounts of what you are spending (your costs) and what you are receiving in revenues. You need this information for yourself, so that you know what your profit is. Even more, though, there is a legal requirement that you should have this evidence available for the taxman.

The difficulty for someone like Tamara is that there are lots of issues to deal with when running a business – staffing to sort out, customers to keep happy, bills to be paid, and so on. Therefore it is easy to push back tax and accounting-related issues until next week...or month.

To make things easier for yourself:

- keep a paper record of what you have to pay out for the business; it helps enormously if you use a business credit/debit card to pay for everything, as this creates its own records of how much you paid and to whom. Try not to pay in cash as it is harder to prove what you spent the money on
- keep a paper record of sales revenue from customers. If your customers get credit (time to pay) make sure to keep track of who has paid and who has not
- keep your own records up to date, probably on a spreadsheet such as Excel
- best of all, budget from the start to have a bookkeeper to come in for half a day a week to do the paperwork for you. This will probably pay for itself in reduced stress and lower tax bills.

When the business starts to grow, there is another tax to consider – VAT (value added tax). Firms with an annual turnover of more than £60,000 (this turnover figure is often increased by the government in the annual budget – to check the latest figure, go to customs.hmrc.gov.uk) have to charge 17.5 per cent VAT to customers, and then pay that money to the government. Failing to register for VAT can be an expensive mistake.

Legal issues

Business organisation

The first legal question is which type of business organisation you want – a limited company or an unlimited firm? Establishing a company creates a separate **legal entity**. In other words, even if Tamara Girvan owned 100 per cent of the shares in Tamara Girvan Ltd, the two would be treated separately in law. If a customer sued after an accident had resulted in her ear being cut, the customer would be suing the business – Tamara Girvan Ltd. If the courts imposed a fine of £100,000 and the business could not pay, Tamara the person would not be liable for the debts of Tamara Girvan Ltd. Therefore if there is any serious risk of legal action, it is wise to form a limited company.

Employment

Every employer has a number of legal responsibilities. The employer's duty of care requires careful thought about Health and Safety at Work, both mental and physical. There are also a series of other laws that need to be complied with, including the Minimum Wage, the Working Time Directive and laws against **discrimination** on grounds of sex, race and age. Therefore every job advertisement has to be thought about carefully. You cannot advertise for 'attractive young waitresses' or 'mature white men'.

Consumer protection

An employer also has clear responsibilities towards customers. The Sale of Goods Act insists that goods should be 'fit for the purpose for which they are sold'. Therefore, if they do not work, customers are legally entitled to get their money back. It is also a requirement that advertisements and pack labels should tell the truth. In fact, telling the truth in pages of small print (as on most financial products) may prove of little help to the customer.

Environmental protection

Employers have environmental responsibilities too. They are required to put waste materials in landfill sites instead of dumping them on the roadside. They must conform to laws about clean air and clean waste water (to avoid polluting rivers). For most small service businesses there are no significant issues here, but for manufacturers they may represent some important and expensive concerns.

Every employer is responsible for health and safety

Conclusion

Starting a business is a massive undertaking. It can lead to a challenging, exciting working life, and can even lead to riches. Yet it is also a massive responsibility. Each year there are more than 100,000 accidents in the workplace. And each year there are people who get food poisoning from restaurants or suffer anxiety from a pension or an investment that was supposed to be safe, but proves not to be. Good businesses look after their staff and their customers because it is the only way to build a successful long-term future. Unfortunately there are also firms that cut corners in their determination to get rich quick. They end up on TV programmes such as *Watchdog* – or in the law courts.

Revision essentials

Discrimination: treating some types of people worse than others for reasons of prejudice.

Legal entity: a person or company that is treated by the law as having its own independent rights and responsibilities.

National Insurance: a form of tax that is paid by employers and employees as a contribution towards welfare payments such as unemployment pay. Employers pay around 13 per cent of the employee's salary.

Exercises

(25 marks; 30 minutes)

Read the unit, then ask yourself:

1. Explain in your own words:
   a) limited company (3)
   b) consumer protection. (3)
2. Why does the text advise against using cash to pay bills? (3)
3. a) What is a bookkeeper for? (2)
   b) Explain how Tamara might have benefited from using a bookkeeper. (4)
4. Identify four faults in these recruitment advertising statements:
   a) Wanted: a recent school-leaver to train as a postman
   b) Wanted: strong, fit Afro-Caribbean waitress for a new bar in Brixton. (4)
5. Given Tamara's achievements with her new business, discuss whether she should have been put off by the problems with the taxman. (6)

Practice questions

(20 marks; 20 minutes)

Michael Woolsey started a printing franchise business at the age of 21. His parents helped him with the start-up capital, but after that he was largely on his own. His father's only piece of advice was to use the government's Business Link service for small firms. This proved invaluable.

When he contacted Business Link through their website (www.businesslink.gov.uk) Michael was offered a free session with a local business advisor. Their meeting went very well, so Michael paid for another session two weeks later. The advisor was especially helpful about accounting software, showing him how to record costs and revenues and to automatically produce profit statements. Michael was warned about the need to keep evidence of money spent on business costs.

After the second meeting Michael started to use the Business Link website more and more. He found a page entitled 'Find out what taxes you need to pay', which he found helpful. Before hiring his first member of staff he went back to the site to read the pages of advice on 'Employing people'.

Two years after starting up, the business (Creovation Ltd) is doing very well. Michael has expanded it to include a website design service and is thinking of opening his second franchise. The success is due to hard work and his positive, warm approach to the four staff and many customers. He is quick to acknowledge, though, that his contacts with Business Link helped him avoid unnecessary and costly mistakes.

SECTION 4 *Making the start-up effective*

Questions

1 Explain how Michael's business would have been helped by the advice on keeping accurate records. (4)

2 a) Identify the evidence that Michael set the business up as a limited company. (1)

   b) Outline two possible benefits of this to Michael. (4)

3 Outline two legal issues Michael should have considered before hiring his first member of staff. (4)

4 To what extent was Michael's success due to Business Link? (7)

29 Effective, on-time delivery

In 2000 the big business story was the internet. A company called **Boo.com** received pages of press coverage as its two founders were young and newsworthy. A company called **Screwfix.com** was hardly mentioned. Yet by 2002 Boo.com had collapsed, while Screwfix sales had risen to over £100 million. There were many differences between the two companies, but the biggest single one was delivery. Screwfix promised to deliver within a day (and did), while Boo.com was famously slack about on-time delivery. Customers felt they came second to the owners' lifestyles, whereas at Screwfix the customer came first.

To deliver on time, every time, is extraordinarily difficult. It requires highly efficient, reliable systems at every stage of the **supply chain**. In November 2005 the **Xbox 360** was launched by Microsoft. The publicity suggested that it was a brilliant success. In fact, only 325,000 360s were sold in November in America. In the same number of days after the launch of the original Xbox, 550,000 units had been sold. The 2005 problem was that Microsoft had failed to supply enough product to meet the demand. As **Sony PS3** would be launched by Christmas 2006, this was a serious delivery failure.

Producing the right number of products at the right time requires four main resources.

1. Sufficient physical capacity. In a restaurant there may only be enough space and enough cookers to be able to produce 30–35 meals an hour. And there may only be enough seats and tables to cope with a maximum of 35 customers at any one time. So the restaurant's physical capacity is 35 an hour. If 40 people arrive, some will have to queue.
2. Enough trained staff. A sudden increase in demand may outstrip the company's ability to hire and train extra staff to get the work done. Even if a firm is not growing, a few absences by staff may make it impossible to get an order completed on time.
3. Capital. A sudden big order can strain a firm's cash flow. Cash has to paid out on supplies and overtime before any cash can come in from the customer. Therefore effective delivery requires extra capital.

4   Effective management. Businesses require different members of staff to work in a coordinated way. It is the job of a manager to establish this coordination and to motivate people to work together.

Together, these four factors are known as land, labour, capital and enterprise.

Even if all four factors are in place, serious problems can still occur. Shocks can disrupt the ability to deliver, and they can come from inside or outside the organisation. A fire at a key supplier can cause chaos. Or bad weather may stop a supplier from being able to deliver to you on time. From inside the business, a strike by your own staff will wreck the ability to supply on time. Machinery breakdowns can cause the same disruption.

Achieving efficient delivery

There are two main requirements.

1   Strong links with customers. A firm needs to be able to forecast the likely level of future demand in order to plan ahead. Close links with consumers should ensure a clear understanding of their purchasing plans (Xbox 360 or PS3?). Large firms also use electronic links with retailers to get the most up-to-date idea of consumer demand. The information recorded every minute by Tesco's till scanners can be fed through so that Danone knows exactly how many Actimels are being bought this morning. This gives a warning of whether tomorrow's order from Tesco will be higher or lower than today's.

2   Commitment throughout the staff. If a promise has been made to a customer, all the staff should be determined not to break it. In a large firm it may be hard to get all the staff to really care about each and every customer; this is where small firms have a major opportunity. At a small TV production company in London, four staff came in on Boxing Day 2005 (unpaid) to complete a commercial that was to have its first showing on 28 December. If people enjoy their job, they will be willing to make extraordinary efforts.

The business benefits

If a firm gets a reputation for reliability and efficiency, it will attract customers. If achieving reliability has required higher-cost production, the higher price of the service will put off some customers. Nevertheless there may be a profitable business targeted at customers willing to pay for reliability. As the table below shows, different airlines perform very differently as regards arriving on time. It looks as if the German airline **Lufthansa** should emphasise its reliability to busy business passengers.

Airline punctuality 2005

	Arrival within 15 minutes	1 hour+ late
Lufthansa	80.77%	2.57%
Ryanair	81.62%	2.44%
BMI	76.41%	2.84%
easyJet	72.05%	5.12%
British Airways	67.57%	5.58%
Monarch Airlines	58.07%	12.87%

(Source: www.flightontime.info analysis of CAA data)

Most important of all is that reliable, on-time delivery encourages **customer loyalty**. This, in turn, gives a firm a more confident basis for operating. If costs rise a little, a firm can push its prices up, knowing that loyal customers will keep coming. Confidence in the loyalty of customers also helps a firm take more risks in investing in its future. In 2005 **Ryanair** announced that it was buying 70 new aircraft from Boeing at a price of $3500 million. It had the confidence to do this as its passenger numbers had grown by 500 per cent between 1999 and 2005.

Conclusion

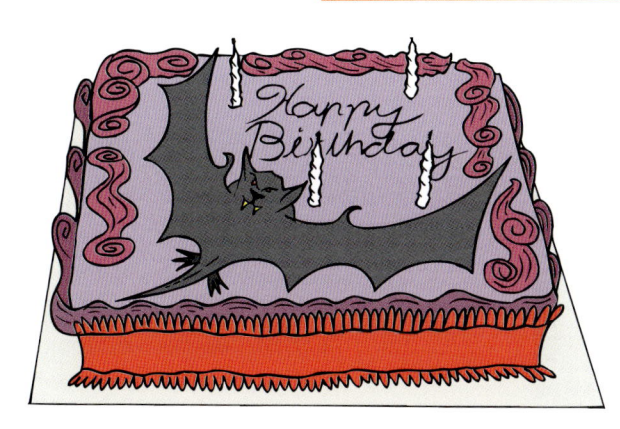

Small firms have many disadvantages compared with larger rivals. On-time delivery, though, can be a major area for competitive advantage. Small firms have greater scope to be flexible and adaptable. If Sharon Osborne desperately needs a table-sized birthday cake to be delivered by 5 p.m. tomorrow, a small firm can produce it and make absolutely sure it gets there on time. **Mr Kipling** would not be able to compete.

Revision essentials

Customer loyalty: buyers returning regularly to buy from the same supplier.

Supply chain: the links in the chain from the start to the end of the supply process. For a bakery that might be: wheat from farm – ground into flour – delivered to baker – baked into bread – sliced and wrapped – delivered to shops.

Exercises

(25 marks; 30 minutes)

Read the unit, then ask yourself:

1. Why will Sony be delighted to hear of Microsoft's supply problems with the Xbox 360? (2)
2. Explain in your own words:
   a) physical capacity (3)
   b) absences by staff. (3)
3. Why may effective, on-time delivery be easier for a business with a clear customer focus? (4)

4 The biggest requirement for on-time delivery in Britain at the moment is to get the Olympic Village ready for 2012. Outline how the managers of the London Olympics should handle the four key factors: land, labour, capital and enterprise. (8)
5 Outline one way in which Lufthansa might make more use of its impressive punctuality figures. (5)

Practice questions (20 marks; 20 minutes)

Food stores in online sales surge

www.bbcnews.com/business, 15 December 2005

Supermarkets with online sites are coming under extra pressure this year as more people try to order their Christmas groceries over the internet. The retail consultancy TNS predicts that Britons will spend £3.3bn next week – a rise of 17 per cent from the same week last year.

The *Financial Times* insisted several supermarkets – Tesco, Asda and Ocado, as well as Sainsbury's – have already stopped taking Christmas orders following a massive rise in demand. The paper quoted Tesco as saying its weekly internet orders had jumped from an average of 170,000 to 200,000 in the past two weeks, leaving its 1500 delivery vans at full capacity.

Other retailers have also said they could do a lot more business if they had the physical capacity to deliver the goods ordered. But the online supermarkets say they alerted regular customers to the potential problems in November and early December and encouraged people to book early.

This was a sensible move, TNS told the BBC, as cash-rich and time-poor customers do not want to be messed around. However, some supermarkets admit they have already had to deal with customer complaints over the lack of delivery capacity. 'If there was a risk of failing to fill the Christmas orders that would be a publicity disaster of heroic proportions', Ed Garner from TNS told BBC News.

Questions

1 Outline one way in which supermarkets such as Tesco might have avoided this situation. (4)
2 Discuss how well the supermarkets seem to have handled the unexpectedly high demand for online shopping. (6)
3 Explain the importance to firms of the statement: 'cash-rich and time-poor customers do not want to be messed around'. (4)
4 Examine two possible effects on a firm of a publicity disaster in relation to Christmas orders. (6)

30 Recruiting the right staff

> *'I don't care if his skills are weak and he's got no experience. Look at that enthusiasm and energy level. He's going to be terrific!'*
> Edgar Trenner, businessman

Salvatore Falcone has run a bakery in Wimbledon for nearly 40 years. In that time he has built Panetteria Italiana into a terrific business. People drive 20 miles to buy armfuls of bread for their freezer. His Saturday morning queue is legendary. Yet in all these years he has rarely been able to find and keep staff. His business works because his wife and three children work there. When he tries to recruit someone, he usually finds the person too slow or too unconcerned to be worth having. He says, 'I take them on, I spend weeks training them up, then they decide to go elsewhere.'

For a small firm, recruiting staff is a worrying process. There is a huge amount that could go wrong. And a small business lacks the expertise to avoid some of the pitfalls. Could the job advertisement be accused of **discrimination**? Is the job interview process unbiased? And does the person being interviewed really want the job, or is s/he just planning to use it as a stepping stone to something better?

The breakthrough

There are nearly 4 million businesses in Britain, but fewer than 1.2 million have any employees. The vast majority are true sole traders, employing no one. The business is run by one person, helped by family members.

The star businesses are those that break away from being purely family firms. They need the courage to hire staff, despite the problems that may result. Every staff member causes a business to pay extra taxes, give four weeks' holiday pay and meet laws that cover health and safety, job security and conditions of work.

The breakthrough comes when employers gain the commitment and confidence to hire people and start treating them like adults. This requires skills that many entrepreneurs lack. They are often good at bossing people about, but poor at encouraging people to think for themselves.

Often small firms start by recruiting friends or former workmates. This gets round any concerns about whether the new recruit will prove unfriendly or work-shy. As a business grows, however, the boss will soon run out of friends to be brought in. Then the real process starts of judging people you do not know. The keys to this process are:

- a CV (**curriculum vitae**), which sets out the person's qualifications, experience and any other relevant facts
- **references**, usually in the form of a letter from a named friend, teacher or colleague, who will write about the applicant's qualities
- an interview, which enables the boss to judge the applicant's personality and his/her attitude to the job on offer (enthusiastic? well prepared? scruffy, with a couldn't-care-less attitude?)
- sometimes, a test on the person's skills (typing ability and speed, perhaps) or their personality.

Small firms should be especially careful about the personalities of the people they recruit. A quiet, dull person may dampen the atmosphere at work, making it harder for people to enjoy coming to work. The table below shows the skills that employers say they are looking for. Usually this is on top of a requirement that candidates should have GCSEs in Maths and English.

> 'Judge a man by his questions, not his answers.'
> Voltaire, French philosopher

Top 10 skills that employers look for

Commercial awareness	Knowing what makes companies tick
Communication	Including presentations and written and verbal communication skills
Teamwork	Proving you're a team player but with the ability to manage others
Negotiation and persuasion	Being able to 'get your way', but also understanding where the other person is coming from
Problem solving	Including analysis and logical thinking
Leadership	Motivating a team and assigning tasks and deadlines
Organisation	Prioritising your workload and time
Ability to meet deadlines	Proving your efficiency and time-management skills
Ability to work under pressure	Keeping calm in a crisis and not becoming too overwhelmed or stressed
Confidence	In yourself, your colleagues and the company

(Source: doctorjob.com)

More of the same?

Entrepreneurs are inclined to recruit people like themselves. It is comfortable to work with people of the same race, from the same area and of the same age. Yet this may cause serious problems for the business. Firms need staff with different points of view, perhaps stemming from different backgrounds. In 2001 the frozen foods business **Iceland** decided to drop its 'buy one get one free' promotional campaign and reposition the business as an organic foods company. Prices went up – and sales plunged. Within six months this daft strategy was reversed. How come no middle manager said beforehand that this was a bad idea? The senior management was too wealthy and too middle class to understand the customers. The business needed some different points of view.

Well-run firms like to have a wide range of different ages, classes and races working for them. This ensures that all possible types of customer can be understood by staff working within the business.

> 'Hiring and training are costly – but it is infinitely more costly to have a barely average man on the company payroll for 30 years.'
> Gordon Wheeling, personnel manager

Conclusion

Firms that aim to grow have no choice but to recruit staff. When they do this they need to be alert to the risks of hiring someone who may be disruptive, yet accept that this is unlikely. Most workers want to do a good job, and should be given the opportunity and encouragement to get on with it.

Revision essentials

Curriculum vitae: the story of life (i.e. a summary of a person's qualifications, achievements and interests).

Discrimination: choosing one type of person in preference to another, perhaps on the grounds of race, sex or age.

References: a letter to support a job application from someone the job applicant has chosen (e.g. a previous boss).

Exercises

(20 marks; 25 minutes)

Read the unit, then ask yourself:

1. Salvatore has had little luck finding staff. Identify two possible reasons why he might be failing to recruit the staff he needs. (2)
2. a) How many British businesses employ no employees at all? (1)
   b) Identify two reasons why businesses may be reluctant to hire staff. (2)

3 Reread the explanation of 'references' (under Revision essentials). Outline one reason why an employer might be cautious about a very positive reference about a job applicant. (2)
4 Explain why a small business should look carefully at the personality of a job applicant. (4)
5 Discuss the importance of recruiting staff from a wide range of social and racial backgrounds to one of the following organisations:
   a) hospital
   b) hairdresser's
   c) dress designer's. (6)
6 Explain in your own words the meaning of Gordon Wheeling's statement: 'Hiring and training are costly – but it is infinitely more costly to have a barely average man on the company payroll for 30 years.' (3)

Practice questions (20 marks; 20 minutes)

Recruitment 'inhibits small firm growth'

One in five small businesses cannot grow their business because of problems recruiting staff, according to research released today.

A report from the Tenon Forum think-tank shows 20 per cent of small businesses feel effective recruitment is the largest barrier to their growth. Larger firms can offer salary and benefit levels which they cannot. Many small businesses are also less likely to have the expertise to find talented staff.

Bigger businesses find recruitment less of an obstacle to growth. Of companies with 5–9 employees, 22 per cent say recruitment is their biggest barrier, compared to 9 per cent of firms with 200–499 employees.

Small firms have a number of distinct benefits that are not always found in larger organisations, said Richard Kennett of the Tenon Foundation. '[Smaller firms offer] earlier opportunities for promotion and career advancement, more job flexibility, more direct personal contact with senior management and a higher profile within the company', Kennett said. 'By increasing awareness of these benefits, small businesses will start to address the issue of recruitment.'

The survey also identified market conditions, cash flow, competition and attitudes to risk were listed as other leading restrictions on the growth of small firms.

(Source: adapted from www.startups.co.uk 16 June 2005)

Questions

1 Outline two reasons why recruitment may be the largest barrier to the growth of small firms. (4)
2 Explain two possible advantages to employees of taking a job in a small firm rather than a large one. (6)
3 Discuss the restrictions on the growth of small firms caused by any one of the following:
   a) market conditions
   b) competition
   c) attitudes to risk. (10)

31 Staff training

In 2002 chef Jamie Oliver set up a charity called **Fifteen**. Its aim was to open a top quality restaurant staffed by young people from difficult backgrounds. One-third of the places on the course would be reserved for teenagers who are homeless or recently out of prison. None would have any previous experience in catering, yet all would be trained to become top-class chefs. It was a dazzlingly ambitious idea.

The Fifteen programme costs the charity £18,000 per trainee, and includes:

- three months at a catering college, learning basic kitchen skills, such as cutting and slicing
- 'sourcing' trips, going to farms in Scotland or vineyards in Italy to learn about the importance of top quality ingredients
- constant emphasis on improving the students' ability to taste the difference between average and delicious foods and wine
- work experience, often at some of London's finest restaurants, such as Le Gavroche, where the standards demanded of the students are incredibly high
- working at Fifteen, spending a week on each section: grill, pasta, pastry, fish, butchery, bakery and as a waiter, to really learn the trade, then a period of time specialising in one section.

Today, Fifteen is a hugely popular restaurant in Hoxton, East London, with all its profits being used to fund the charity. It is working with its fourth group of students, and its graduates are working in great restaurants around the world. There is an equally successful Fifteen in Amsterdam, and there will soon be one in Cornwall and another in Australia. The whole project is based on Jamie Oliver's view that everyone deserves great training.

SECTION 4 *Making the start-up effective*

One of the first graduates from Fifteen, Asher Wyborn, said:

One of the biggest lessons I'll take with me is that you don't need to treat people badly to get results. I hope none of us become like the old-style breed of chefs that treat people like scum because that's how they were treated on the way up. This place has shown me that respect breeds respect and it's something I'll take with me wherever I go.

Why train?

If a job was so simple that it required no training, it probably could – and would – be done by a robot. Yet there is much more to training than telling people how to do a job. Well-run organisations keep investing in staff training because there is no limit to the amount to be learned. Take, for example, the reasons why experienced teachers might need training:

- to know about a new GCSE course, or a change to an existing one;
- to be kept up to date by the chief examiner about the latest thinking in how the exams are to be set and marked;
- to learn about new technology available for teaching, perhaps downloadable from the internet.

In other words, things change, and training is a way to keep people on top of their job. This should ensure high-quality staff performance, and also helps staff feel properly looked after by the business, which boosts morale and motivation.

Induction

> 'Train everyone – lavishly… You can't overspend on training.'
> Tom Peters, management guru

When you join an organisation, there is always some **induction** training, to ease you into the job. Simple induction tasks include being shown the fire exits and the canteen and being introduced to colleagues. A more ambitious programme will include:

- a presentation by a director on the aims and plans of the business
- a detailed explanation of the role of the department you are working for
- perhaps, as at Fifteen, a programme of spending a week in different departments, to get a broad understanding of the business.

For a new, young employee, the length (and therefore cost) of the induction programme is a good indication of how seriously the management treats your appointment. If, as at Fifteen, you are flown off to Italy for part of the programme, you would be right to feel special.

Training

'The more a person can do, the more you can motivate them...that's the point of training.'
Professor Herzberg, academic

Training can be **on-the-job** or **off-the-job**. Both have an important role to play in most businesses. A new recruit at **Tesco** might learn to use the till on-the-job, helped by a supervisor. Later, though, if there is a chance of promotion, off-the-job training may take place at a local college. This training might be in people skills, such as persuasion, or in IT skills, such as using the company's spreadsheet system of recording stock wastage (theft plus stock thrown away as it passes its sell-by date).

The most important aspect of training, though, is whether it is aimed at the attitudes and personal skills of the individual, or whether it is solely for a practical purpose. A Tesco supervisor might be put on a training course on 'Using the new Tesco stock control system'. This is fine, but it is purely for Tesco's benefit. Well-run companies also encourage staff to pursue training programmes that develop the person. For example, shy people might be encouraged to go on an assertiveness training course. This would teach them to be stronger and firmer when dealing with others (including their boss). Many firms allocate a sum of money per employee, allowing the individual to follow any course they would like (e.g. learning to speak Spanish or play the piano). The companies do this because they want to be seen to invest in their staff. Tesco has long had an excellent reputation for this type of personal development as well as purely business-focused training.

Is training always a good thing?

'All genuine knowledge originates in direct experience.'
Mao Tse-Tung, Chinese leader

Training, like teaching, is a good thing unless it is boring or seems irrelevant. Large firms are likely to prepare training programmes for all their staff. There may be a section on health and safety that is vital to some and means nothing to others; or a section on equal opportunities at work that many feel is stating the obvious – that there is no place at work for prejudice on grounds of race, age or sex.

To be effective, training programmes need to be tailored to individual needs. A part-time worker wondering about a career may welcome the opportunity to go on a training course on supervisory skills. Another may only be interested in Friday's pay cheque and therefore hate 'boring' training. Good managers know their staff well enough to know who wants what, and why.

Revision essentials

Induction: initial training to make newcomers feel comfortable in their new job.
Off-the-job: training that takes place away from the job (e.g. at college or at a company's training centre).
On-the-job: training that takes place while working at the job (e.g. till training at a supermarket).

Exercises

(20 marks; 25 minutes)

Read the unit, then ask yourself:

1. When they are finally graded, Jamie Oliver's programme judges each student on four key factors: attendance, skills, effort and attitude. Briefly outline the importance of any two of these factors to an employer. (4)
2. The training programme at Fifteen takes 14 months, whereas a new employee at a fast-food restaurant might get only a day's training before starting work. Discuss how employees at Fifteen are likely to feel about their job compared with those starting at the burger bar. (6)
3. Give two reasons why a firm should run an induction programme. (2)
4. Sam Allardyce, the football manager, has taken a lot of off-the-job training, including a course on management at Warwick University. Outline two ways in which he might benefit from this. (4)
5. 'Staff training would be a waste of money, as half my staff leave within a year.' Explain to this business owner two reasons why s/he should change this attitude to training. (4)

Practice questions

(20 marks; 20 minutes)

No concerns over staff treatment here – this company's Innocent

It's not every day that a food and drink company has people begging to work for them. But take a quick glance at the website of smoothie and juice maker Innocent Drinks: 'I may be only a lowly student but PLEASE give me a job! I worship you all.'

The creation of a company with such a glowing personnel record has certainly not been down to chance. Innocent was set up back in 1999 when three friends, disillusioned with the tedium of their working lives, decided to form a company that would not only make them money but that would bring some fun back into their lives. Just under six years on, and while the business has grown to now employ 50 staff – 47 full-time and three 'really nice helpers' – its attitudes have remained the same.

Take the company's induction process. New recruits are given a two-week timetable of meetings with *every* member of staff to give a picture of what they do. In addition to this, the company runs what it calls its lunchmate programme, which for the first two weeks assigns a different member of staff each day as a lunch partner.

This simple yet personal approach to ensure staff are well looked after is the essence of Innocent's management. Co-founder Adam Bolan says, 'We want to be Europe's favourite little juice company. Little is about attitude, not size.' It recognises that small gestures can be just as effective as the grand ones. 'You don't have to do big flashy things to motivate staff and keep them happy. It is the little things that matter the most.' Among these 'little things' is an annual allowance of up to £2000 that staff can spend on training on any topic they want.

(Source: adapted from *Food Manufacture* magazine, William Reed, 7 February 2005)

Questions

1 From the article, identify two reasons why the 'lowly student' might be begging for a job at Innocent. (2)
2 Comment on the likely benefits to new staff of Innocent's induction process. (5)
3 Adam Bolan highlights the importance of 'little things that matter the most' to staff. Discuss the advantages and disadvantages to Innocent of its generous training allowance to its staff. (8)
4 Explain why a small business such as Innocent might find it easier to provide good training than a huge firm such as Coca-Cola. (5)

32 Motivation

A reward for a motivated entrepreneur

Motivation matters. Motivation matters massively. In January 2006 Burton Albion played Manchester United in the FA Cup third round. Playing at home, the part-timers of Burton outfought and even outplayed United. Even when Wayne Rooney came on with half an hour to go, Burton looked the more motivated side. The game ended nil-nil, providing Burton with a £500,000 jackpot in a replay at Old Trafford. Motivation allows small companies to outperform large ones, and employees of average ability to outperform cleverer ones.

At 3.30 a.m. on a Saturday morning, Salvatore Falcone starts work at his bakery. He makes and bakes bread, pizzas, doughnuts, cakes and pastries until 11.30 a.m., then serves customers until 4.30 in the afternoon. On a Sunday evening he races stock cars at Wimbledon race track, often winning in this fast, dangerous sport. In return for his amazing motivation, he has been able to afford houses in London and Italy, and is now eyeing a soft-top Ferrari Testarrossa. He works hard, plays hard and is about as happy a man as you could find.

Entrepreneurs have motivation, but the big question is: how to motivate staff who are not getting the direct financial reward from the success of the business?

What exactly *is* motivation?

To most people, motivation simply means having the commitment to do something. Within the home, it may be decorating the bathroom; at work, it may be working late to finish a job. However, Professor Herzberg says that motivation is doing something because you *want* to do it. In other words, motivation is not about whether you do it, it is why and how you do it. Motivation, he says, does not come from money or from threats ('do this, or else'); it only comes from within.

There are many possible ways to motivate staff. Among them are:

- giving them a real sense of purpose. Staff on a hospital maternity ward should be fine, but in a profit-making business it may be harder. Yet high quality standards can motivate people, as can success. Employees of Apple loved seeing iPod beating Sony and taking 75 per cent of the market for MP3 players
- involving them in the decisions made by the business (e.g. getting shop-floor staff involved in deciding how to rearrange the shop to encourage higher sales)
- giving them meaningful, challenging tasks. An American TV station asked its staff to come up with a new schedule of programmes for a Friday night. The management followed the advice of staff and the viewing audience rose 20 per cent. The staff then reorganised the rest of the week's programmes with equal success – and the number of staff days off 'sick' fell by 30 per cent.

Is money not a motivator?

Everyone agrees that pay is a crucial part of staff satisfaction. People work in order to earn money, and if they feel underpaid they leave. That is not the same as saying that pay makes people work harder or better. A head of department may earn 35 per cent more than an ordinary teacher. Does that make him/her work 35 per cent harder? Or even any harder at all? Probably not.

Of course, money can be used to make people work faster. A bricklayer who lays 500 bricks a day could be offered a £30 bonus for laying an extra 100 bricks in the time. Almost certainly the bricklayer will work faster to achieve the bonus. The risk is that this will be at the cost of poorer-quality bricklaying.

Professor Herzberg explains that money can get people to work faster or longer, but people produce the best work when they are motivated; and motivation comes from within. Motivation is doing it because you want to.

What should managers do to motivate their staff?

In a small firm it should be quite easy to ensure that most staff are well motivated. The boss should:

- train staff so that they feel confident doing what they are asked to do
- give them meaningful jobs to do, with opportunities to show their ability
- talk to them regularly to make sure they know what is happening now and what is planned for the future

- give them the opportunity to contribute ideas; and then act on the good ones
- pay fairly, so that someone who is contributing a lot is given pay rises to reflect his/her achievements and efforts.

What are the benefits of a motivated staff?

High morale and motivation rubs off on customers. They feel better about the company and therefore keep coming back. This is especially important in businesses where staff see the customers every day, such as a waiter, a hotel receptionist or a school teacher. High motivation is also likely to lead to:

- lower **absenteeism** (i.e. very few staff taking days off work)
- lower **labour turnover**, with fewer staff looking for other jobs and therefore fewer leaving. As recruiting staff is expensive, it saves a huge amount if staff stay loyal
- improved teamwork within the business; this encourages more ideas to come from staff discussions that may lead to major business benefits.

> 'In order that people be happy in their work, these three things are needed: they must be fit for it; they must not do too much of it; and they must have a sense of success in it.'
>
> John Ruskin, philosopher

Conclusion

The most successful companies are usually those with the best-motivated staff. People who have started their own business can underestimate the importance of this. They often expect people to find the motivation from within, without doing enough to create a situation in which staff can easily be motivated. If the boss barks out orders and hands over a series of dull tasks, it is no surprise if staff dislike their work. Motivation requires a manager to think how to organise work so that staff can feel that their intelligence is being used properly.

> **Revision essentials**
> **Absenteeism:** the percentage of the workforce that is absent on the average day. The national average is about 3 per cent, but in some organisations it is as high as 10 per cent.
> **Labour turnover:** the percentage of the workforce that leaves each year and has to be replaced.

Exercises

(20 marks; 25 minutes)

Read the unit, then ask yourself:

1. Why may it be harder for entrepreneurs to motivate their staff than it is to motivate themselves? (3)
2. In 2003 Claude Makelele left the world's most glamorous team, Real Madrid, to join Chelsea. Although he earned over £1 million a year at Real, he felt unfairly treated compared with the star names such as Ronaldo. So he left. For the following three years Madrid won nothing.
   a) Outline two reasons why firms should treat every member of staff fairly. (4)
   b) Explain why a firm should be worried if its labour turnover is too high. (4)
3. Why may Professor Herzberg believe that money is not a motivator? (3)
4. Identify two reasons why training staff may improve their motivation. (2)
5. Explain two ways in which a firm might benefit from lower absenteeism. (4)

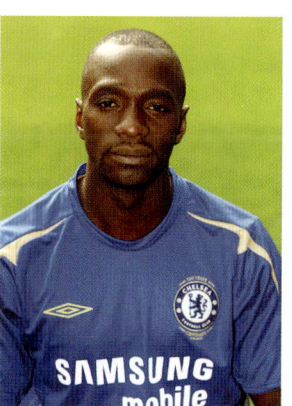

Practice questions

(20 marks; 20 minutes)

Building a building business

Jensens Engineering was founded in 1993. It designs, builds and installs heating, ventilation and air-conditioning equipment throughout the UK. The company has 50 employees. It supplies the building trade, which is one of the most dangerous trades to work in.

The challenge

The company's directors were concerned about a high rate of staff turnover and the effect this was having on projects, availability of skills and profits. Despite being paid competitive salaries, people still moved on and the morale of those who remained was low. The whole company approach had to change in order to maintain its reputation and growth.

The strategy

The directors aimed to give all employees a greater feeling for the company through greater involvement in their day-to-day work. Managers started to meet each member of staff once a fortnight instead of once a year. Identifying and taking action on training and development was supported by generous budgets, especially on health and safety.

The result

Staff turnover has been reduced by over 70 per cent. Similarly, absenteeism has been slashed. Sales turnover doubled in the following three years. Sales and profits improved significantly year on year. The way the organisation now works, and what its people feel about it has changed beyond recognition. 'The pay cheque is important, but it's the job that's the trophy.'

SECTION 4 *Making the start-up effective*

Questions

1 How might a high rate of staff turnover affect profits at Jensens Engineering? (4)
2 When morale is bad, it is usually the most highly skilled staff who leave, as they can find another job quite easily. Outline two effects on a firm of losing its most highly skilled staff. (4)
3 Why may Jensens management have decided to meet each staff member once a fortnight? (4)
4 Discuss the causes and effects of Jensen's efforts to improve the motivation of their staff. (8)

SECTION 5

UNDERSTANDING THE ECONOMIC CONTEXT

33 Introduction to the economic context

Even if you make good decisions at every key point, starting up a new business is difficult. Making it harder still are factors outside any manager's control. Many stem from changes to the economy. For instance, a slowdown in the economy may lead to rising unemployment. If people are out of work (or feel the threat of unemployment), they cut back their spending, especially on luxuries. This may lead to a sharp decline in takings at restaurants, jewellers and pricier shops.

Many businesses start up when times are good, and it seems easy to make money from free-spending customers. It is important to remember, though, that hard times can be around the corner. This should be okay as long as you have thought how to respond to an economic downturn. During the 1990–92 **recession**, many commentators suggested that Richard Branson's **Virgin** group was about to collapse. In fact he came through that period stronger than ever.

What is the economy?

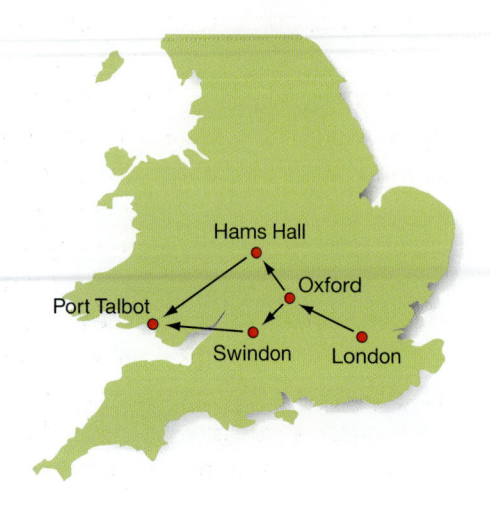

The economy as a series of connected loops

The British economy is the collection of business transactions that takes place throughout the country, throughout the year. If you add up the value of all the goods and services produced in Britain in a year, the total figure comes to over £1 trillion (£1,000,000,000,000). 'The economy' is made up of lots of companies buying and selling with each other, lots of firms selling directly to customers (some here and some overseas) and lots of money raised by and spent by the government.

The key to understanding the economy is to see it as a series of connected loops. If I buy a new **MINI Cooper** in London, I pay £15,000 to the dealer. Yet that triggers a series of payments to: Oxford (where the car was made); Swindon (where the steel body panels were made); Hams Hall, Warwickshire (where the engine was made); Port Talbot, South Wales (where the steel was made); and so on. In fact, over 2000 suppliers are involved in producing every MINI, and they come from Scotland and the North-East as well as in the areas immediately around Oxford. The higher the demand for MINIs, the greater the injection of money and jobs into the veins of the national economy. As workers become more confident of their future prospects (secure job, good income etc.), they become more willing to spend – perhaps on a new MINI. Greater prosperity feeds on itself, creating an upward spiral.

Needless to say, if things start to go wrong, the reverse happens. During an economic downturn there is a downward spiral of falling confidence and lower spending. Cutbacks by customers in London can have knock-on effects in Oxford, Swindon, Scotland, and so on.

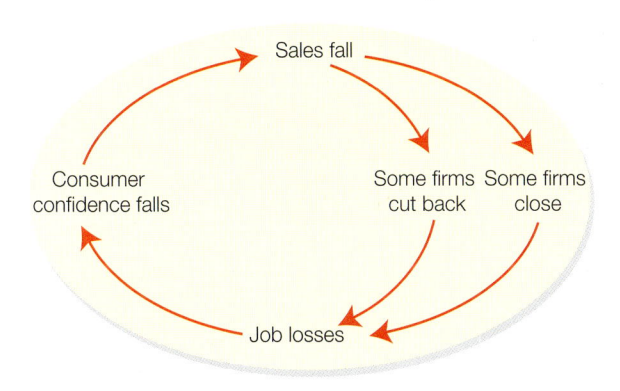

Recession – the downward spiral

What makes the economy go up and down?

It is important to remember that Britain is one of the world's most open economies. Trade with other countries accounts for more than 30 per cent of the value of all goods and services produced in Britain per year. Therefore if America gets flu, we catch a cold. Cutbacks by American consumers would hurt our large companies in banking, insurance and car production, all of which rely on **exports**. Poor economic conditions in Europe hit us even harder, as more than 50 per cent of all British exports are to European Union countries such as France and Germany.

Problems can also hit the economy from within the country. In 2004, house prices were rising so fast that the Bank of England decided to make it harder for people to afford to pay such high prices. The Bank put interest rates up, making mortgages more expensive and therefore cutting down the level of house buying. The rise in interest rates made people more reluctant to use their credit cards in 2005, and the growth of the economy slowed down to its lowest level for 10 years.

145

What do businesspeople most need to know about the economy?

The way interest rates can change

The interest rate is the amount a lender charges per year to someone who has borrowed money. It is measured as a percentage, for example 8 per cent – in other words, the borrower has to pay the lender £8 per year for every £100 borrowed. In addition, the lender must pay the £100 back, perhaps on a monthly basis.

In early 2006 banks charged between 8 and 10 per cent for money borrowed to finance a business start-up. There have been times before when the rate has risen as high as 15 or even 20 per cent, making it very hard to afford the repayments. Whenever possible it is wise to get the bank to agree to a fixed interest rate, so there are no nasty surprises.

The way exchange rates can change

The exchange rate is the value of the £, measured by how much foreign currency can be bought per £. For instance, in March 2005 £1 could be exchanged for $1.90 when travelling to America. By November 2005 the £ had fallen, so that it was worth just $1.70. For a British tourist, the lower exchange rate would dampen the shopping thrills of New York. For **Rolls-Royce**, selling a £50 million aero-engine to an American airline, the stakes are higher. A falling £ makes UK exports more profitable.

The firms who would be most concerned about changes to the £'s exchange rate are:

- big importers, such as electrical goods companies or car showrooms
- big exporters, such as Rolls-Royce, who export more than 90 per cent of the products they make; for Rolls-Royce, a higher £ squeezes the profitability of their exports
- UK producers competing in the UK against foreign companies (e.g. JCB excavators, which has to compete directly against the Japanese Komatsu and the US firm Caterpillar).

The threat of recession

During the big recession of 1990–92, 3 million workers were put out of work and thousands of businesses collapsed. Furthermore many people lost their houses when they could not afford to keep up with their mortgages. A few firms succeeded despite the difficulties, such as the discount shops **Matalan**, **Lidl** and **Aldi**. For most, though, it was a nightmare.

A recession is a severe downturn in the economy, often described as when economic activity falls for two successive quarters of the year.

Firms can usually expect that **consumer spending** will grow a little each year, perhaps about 2.5 per cent. When spending actually falls, companies struggle to cope with falling revenues and cash inflows. Well-run companies look ahead, both to check that no recession is looming and to make sure that they can cope if one arrives. For instance, when the 2005 consumer slowdown hit Whitbread's **David Lloyd** health club business, the company was helped out by the strong showing of its low-priced hotel chain **Travelodge**.

> **Revision essentials**
> **Consumer spending:** the total spent by all shoppers throughout the country.
> **Exports:** goods produced in one country but sold overseas (e.g. a British-made Mini sold in France).
> **Recession:** a downturn in sales and output throughout the economy, often leading to rising unemployment.

Exercises

(A and B: 25 marks; 30 minutes)

A Read the unit, then ask yourself:

1 Give two examples of transactions where one business would sell to another business. (2)
2 Explain what the text means by 'an upward spiral'. (3)
3 Explain why the Bank of England put interest rates up in 2004. (3)
4 If a small British firm wanted to start exporting for the first time, would it prefer the £ to be high and rising or weak and falling? Briefly explain your answer. (5)

B Exports smash through £10 billion barrier

Students often ask: what does Britain export? A surprising answer is food. In 2005, for the first time, British exports of Food and Drink beat £10,000 million. Many of the success stories were small firms such as Ilchester Cheese Company and Welsh Exporter of the Year: Anglesey Sea Salt. 2005 was a good year partly because the value of the £ was not quite as high against the euro. This meant that it was easier for British firms to sell goods to countries in the Eurozone such as Italy, Spain and France. Exports were also helped by higher consumer spending in much of Europe.

(Source: *The Grocer*, 17 December 2005)

1 Outline two possible benefits to small firms of finding export markets for their goods. (4)
2 Outline two reasons why British food exports rose in 2005. (4)
3 Small firms usually charge higher prices in export markets than in Britain. Explain why that might be necessary in order to make exporting profitable. (4)

Unit 33 Introduction to the economic context

Practice questions

(25 marks; 25 minutes)

2005 retail sales collapse to 22-year low

High streets continued to look like ghost towns in June 2005, as newly released sales figures show the sharpest annual drop in receipts in 22 years. A monthly survey of retailers [shopkeepers] found that 42% said their sales volumes were down over the year to June, while just 23% said they were up. The resulting negative 19% balance marks the largest annual drop in sales recorded since this survey began in 1983.

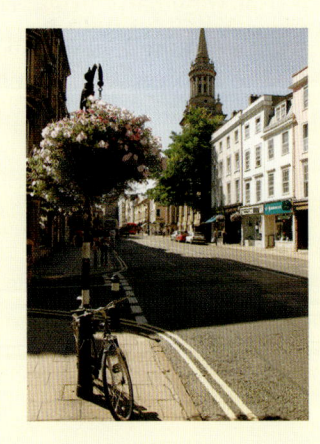

'There is no doubt that the underlying picture is bad', said an Asda sales director. 'Last year's interest rate rises were, as usual, slow to take effect, but consumers have clearly tightened their belts quite significantly since the beginning of this year.'

The director said that many stores have brought forward their summer sales in an attempt to encourage shoppers to open their wallets.

The report is expected to add pressure on the Bank of England to cut interest rates. The British Retail Consortium (BRC) said the sharp year-on-year fall highlights the worsening trading conditions and said the situation will worsen if the Bank fails to act. 'Even City economists have now come around to our view that a significant cut in rates is essential to prevent further deterioration', said BRC director general Kevin Hawkins.

(Source: www.startups.co.uk)

Questions

1 Why might consumers 'tighten their belts' when interest rates rise? (3)
2 Outline how a general fall in UK consumer spending might affect:
   a) Rococo, a small business making and selling luxury chocolates (5)
   b) T. Hughes, a small bakery with loyal, local customers. (5)
3 Outline two ways in which worried retailers might respond to low sales figures. (4)
4 Even when consumer spending is generally poor, some shops maintain high sales of expensive items. Discuss two factors that are likely to be important in achieving this success. (8)

34 Demand and supply

Demand

Most small business decisions are made with little real certainty about the circumstances and the effects. When a minicab firm decides to increase the price it charges from Oxford to Heathrow Airport to £36, it may not know all the prices charged by all its rivals; and will certainly not know how the rivals will respond. Will they increase their prices as well? Or will they fight rough by holding prices down (making it hard for the firm to get business)?

For a **market** trader the situation is easier. If s/he starts the day with strawberries priced at £2.50 a kilo and they are not selling, s/he cuts the price to £1.50 and sees what happens. If sales jump ahead, creating a threat that they will be sold out by lunchtime, the trader can quietly slip the price up to £2.20. In this way, the trader can end up creating what is called a demand curve. This is a diagram showing the level of customer demand for a product at different price levels. (See figure, left.)

Drawn out on a piece of graph paper, a demand curve shows not only the known levels of demand at different prices, but also gives an idea about the likely sales at other price points. On the figure on the left, for example, if the trader had 150 punnets left and just an hour before the market closes, s/he would know that a price cut to £1 per kilo would be needed.

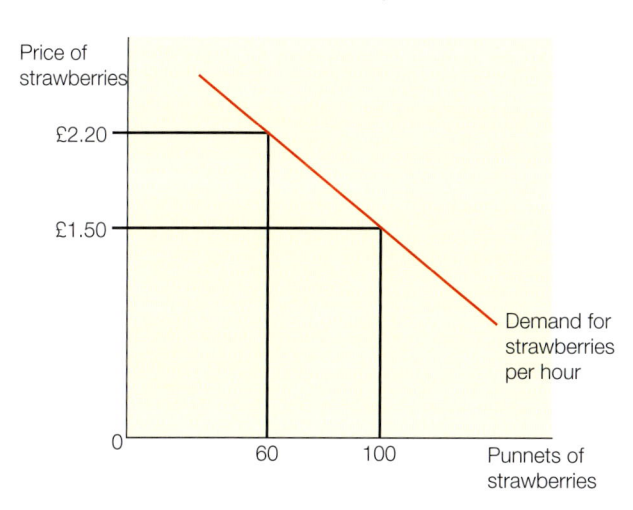

Demand curve for strawberries on a market stall

How useful are demand curves?

They are useful whenever they can be drawn up. The problem is finding out the information. A market stall trader can experiment every hour of every day. It is not possible for **BMW**, though, to offer their 5-Series for £40,000 one month and £30,000 the next (to find out the effect on demand). Customers would not understand what is going on, and there would be a risk of damage to BMW's image.

The most important type of demand curve is one for a **commodity** such as oil. Every day, hundreds of millions of pounds are spent on oil. The lower the price being charged, the higher the level of demand. In the City of London many businesses make a living from buying at a low price one day and selling at a higher price the day after. They need a clear idea of the link between price and demand.

Supply

In markets, price is not only affected by demand, but also by supply. In a street market, if there was a day when only one stall sold strawberries, that stall would have a local **monopoly**. It would be the only supplier of the fruit. If there were not many strawberries available to the market shoppers, the one seller would soon start to sell out. The natural reaction would therefore be to put the price up. If an increase from £1.50 to £2.20 still did not stop customers coming, the trader would push prices up further. In other words, the lower the supply the higher prices will rise.

For a large firm such as **Mars**, an increase in demand for Maltesers would lead the company to produce more, perhaps by getting staff to work overtime. In some circumstances, though, it is impossible to increase supply in the short term. Chelsea season tickets are in great demand, but the supply is limited by the 40,000 capacity of Stamford Bridge. This limited level of supply enables Chelsea to charge some of the world's highest prices for watching football. In a street market, the day's fruit is bought **wholesale** in the early hours of the morning, so there is no possibility of getting extra supply within the day's market trading.

The overall message is simple: a supply shortage leads to high prices; plentiful supply causes prices to fall. Nevertheless, what every supplier wants is high prices. The higher the price, the more enthusiastic s/he will be to supply. This is shown in the figure on the left, in which a supplier will happily supply 100 punnets when the price is £1.50, but only 60 punnets if the price is £1.

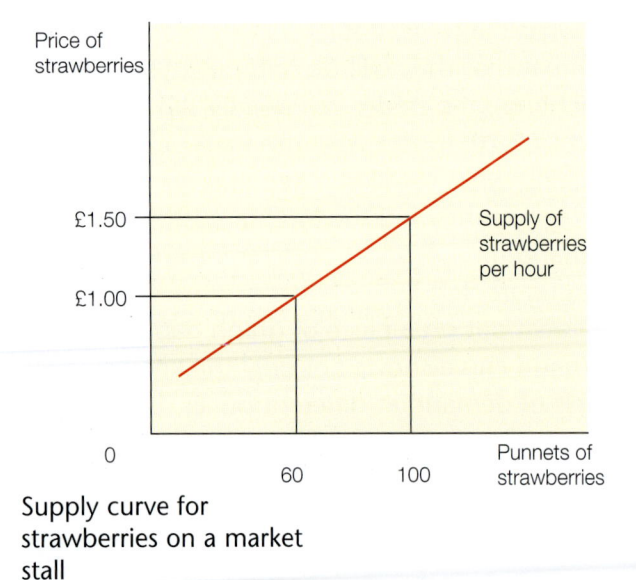

Supply curve for strawberries on a market stall

When supply and demand are in balance

Day by day the prices of many commodities change relatively little. This is because supply and demand are broadly in balance. In other words,

Supply and demand curves for strawberries on a market stall

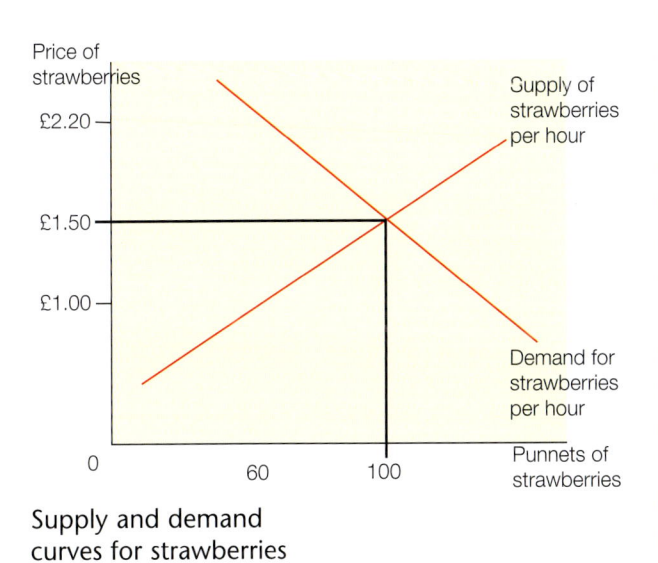

the demand for the item is in line with the amount available. In a situation where demand and supply are matched, the price of the item should be quite stable. Heinz can forecast sales of baked beans with some accuracy, and therefore produces enough to meet the demand. Shop shelves are neither overloaded with beans, nor short of them.

A situation of balance between demand and supply is shown in the figure on the left. Note that the diagram suggests that a selling price of £1.50 is about right. If the price were less than £1.50 there would be plenty of demand, but too few sellers would be willing to supply. If the price was higher than £1.50 the demand would be lower than the amount supplied, leading to rotting, unsold fruit.

What if supply and demand are not in balance?

Small firms need to understand that the prices of key products may vary dramatically with changes in supply and demand. In late 2003 the price of copper was $1600 per tonne. Two years later it was $4600. The price difference was due to rising demand at a time when copper mines were struggling to increase output. Many a plumber could have been caught out by unexpectedly high prices for copper pipes.

Conclusion

Supply and demand determine price in a series of markets, especially those where there are no real differences between the products supplied. The price of Maltesers is decided on by Mars. Yet for a commodity such as copper, high demand can cause prices to shoot ahead, as can a shortage of supply. Clever entrepreneurs make sure to understand what influences the price of everything they buy, to avoid being caught out.

Revision essentials
Commodity: a product in which all supplies are the same, such as a pound of sugar. By contrast, types of jam have different flavours and different brand names.
Market: where buyers and sellers come together; it could be in a particular street, or at an internet location (such as eBay).
Monopoly: where sales in the market are dominated by a single supplier.
Wholesaler: the middleman between producers and retailers; retailers can buy at discounts when they buy wholesale, and may pass that discount on to the public.

Exercises

(20 marks; 25 minutes)

Read the unit, then ask yourself:

1. In the figure on page 149 (Demand curve for strawberries on a market stall), how much revenue would be made per hour by selling at £1.50? And how much at £2.20? (4)
2. Outline two ways in which a firm might use the information found in a demand curve for their key product. (4)
3. In 2006 Arsenal FC increases its seat capacity from 36,000 to 60,000. Outline two possible disadvantages of this to the club. (4)
4. Explain what would happen to a commodity if its demand were higher than its supply. (4)
5. Firms love to lead a predictable life. Why would that be easier for a monopoly supplier than for one operating in a competitive market? (4)

Practice questions

(20 marks; 25 minutes)

2005 saw some dramatic changes in sales of food and drink. Most were influenced by the strong desire by consumers for healthier choices. Walkers Crisps were hit hard, with a fall in sales from £411 million in 2004 to £382 million in 2005. A similar fate hit the soft drink Sunny D, with sales down 19 per cent in response to press criticism of the 'unhealthy' product. By contrast, Innocent Drinks saw colossal sales growth, from £10 million in 2004 to £30.5 million in 2005. Its fruit smoothies are seen as healthy and fun.

Questions

1. **a)** Calculate the percentage decline in sales of Walkers crisps in 2005. (3)
   b) Outline two possible ways Walkers might respond to this fall in demand. (4)
2. Bananas are a key ingredient for Innocent Drinks' smoothies. In 2005 they rose in price by 25 per cent. What changes to the supply of and demand for bananas might have caused this sharp price rise? (4)
3. **a)** By what percentage did Innocent's sales rise in 2005? (3)
   b) Examine two possible causes of this sales increase. (6)

35 Prices in commodity markets

The prices of many of the goods sold in the high street are set by producers and shopkeepers. The latest **Nokia** model is priced by Nokia, not by 'the market'. Yet there are many markets where the producers have no control over the prices. If an oil producer sets the price of its oil at 10 per cent more than the market price, it will not sell any. So the sellers of commodities such as oil have to understand – and respond to – the market.

Commodities include:

- metals such as steel (cars), copper (housing and electronics) and aluminium (cans and also for making aircraft)
- clothing materials, such as cotton, wool and man-made products such as nylon
- food, such as coffee, cocoa and sugar.

The key characteristic of a commodity is that the products are interchangeable. In other words, you can swap one pound of sugar for another, without noticing any difference. Therefore it does not matter who you buy from. Contrast this with football season tickets. Are Manchester United and Manchester City tickets interchangeable? Not according to the customers – the fans. So sugar is a commodity, but season tickets are not.

Supply and demand

The price of a commodity depends on supply and demand. As shown in the figure below, the price will be where supply and demand are in balance. In this case, it is at a figure of $60 per barrel of oil and a sales volume of 70 million barrels per day.

If oil companies want to buy more than 70 million barrels a day the price of oil will rise, possibly quite sharply. In the longer term that may put people off buying oil-based products such as petrol and plastic. Therefore demand will fall back towards its starting point.

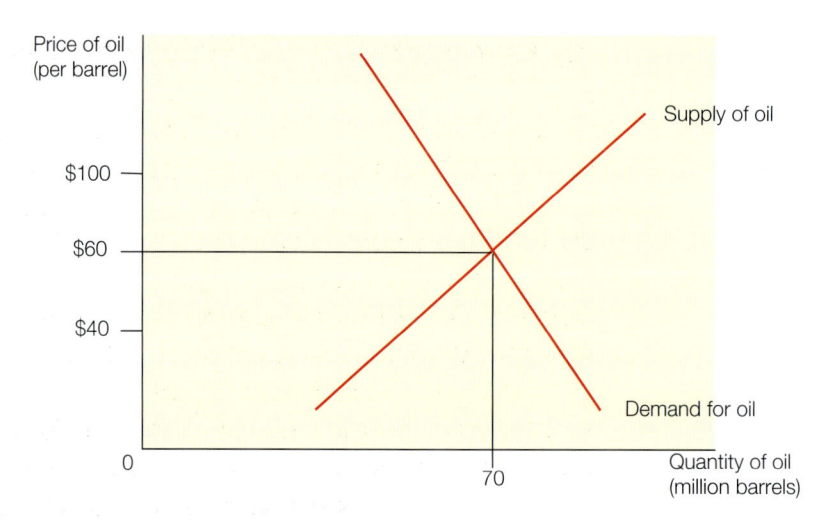

Supply and demand for oil in the world market

Causes of changes in demand for a commodity are:

- a change in the rate of **economic growth**. If the world economy is growing more rapidly than before, demand will rise for almost every commodity. For example, more steel will be bought in order to build more cars. This, in turn, will push up the price of steel
- a change in technology, which may change demand. For example, the new Boeing 'Dreamliner' plane will be made with a new, super-strong carbon fibre instead of aluminium. So demand will fall for aluminium
- a change in buying behaviour. Current consumer attitudes to diet have meant a big drop in demand for sugar, as manufacturers switch to artificial sweeteners such as Splenda. In Britain, Diet Coke now outsells Coke. This has cut the demand for raw sugar – hitting the price obtained by sugar farmers in many developing countries.

Causes of change in the supply of a commodity are:

- if the price of a commodity has been low for some time, suppliers will stop investing in it. For instance, copper prices were low during the 1990s, so the owners of copper mines stopped developing new mines, even when old ones were running out of copper. Then, when the rapid growth of China pushed up the demand for copper in 2004 and 2005, it was impossible to respond quickly by increasing supply. Therefore prices rose sharply
- changes in technology, which can also affect supply. New types of seed, perhaps backed by new fertilisers, may boost the level of supply per acre of land. Chemicals have also been used to boost milk yields. The average cow gave 3000 litres of milk a year in the 1940s. Today it is around 7500 litres (to the concern of many animal welfare groups). Rising supply pushes milk prices down, especially as consumer demand for milk (and cream) is weak.

Is money a commodity?

In the **foreign exchange markets** money is a commodity. In other words, the £ is bought and sold, just as copper is bought and sold. The 'price' of a £ is measured in terms of foreign currency; for example, in January 2006 £1 could be bought for $1.75.

Given that £s can be bought and sold, the market price depends on supply and demand. If lots of Americans want £s in order to travel to Britain for the 2012 Olympics, demand for the £ will rise. Therefore the £ will rise in value. Perhaps it might rise to $1.85 per £. This higher price will make it more expensive for Americans to stay in Britain. It might even put people off coming, which will allow the £'s value to slip back.

The graph below shows the ups and downs of the £ against the $ over the period 1 January 1990 to 2006. Where the line goes up, the £ is rising against the $. This will be because of rising demand for the £ in the foreign exchange markets.

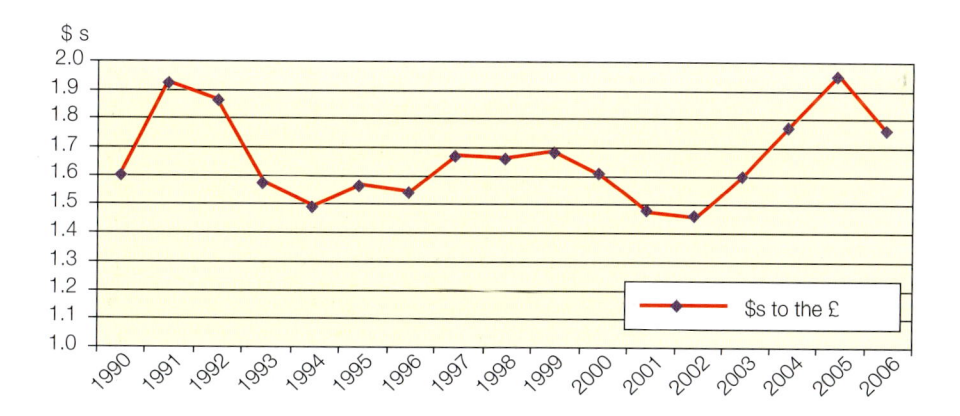

US $ to the £, 1990–2006

Conclusion

Prices of commodities can be very erratic, jumping around due to changes in demand and supply. Firms that use commodities, such as car manufacturers and food producers, need to plan for the worst. Even if the world price of coffee is low at the moment, producers of instant coffee should prepare for it rising in future (perhaps by buying extra supplies when the prices are low). For businesses that produce commodities, such as farmers, erratic prices are scary. If the price of wheat fell by 40 per cent next year, a specialist wheat farmer might struggle to survive. This is why systems exist such as Europe's Common Agricultural Policy (CAP). The CAP controls the price of many agricultural products within the **European Union** so that the farmers know the prices they will receive for their sugar, milk or wheat

Revision essentials

Economic growth: the rate of rise in total output per year within an economy. This rate will determine how wealthy the country becomes in the future.

European Union: the group of 25 European countries that trade freely with one another and have agreements on many areas of social and economic policy.

Foreign exchange markets: the places where currencies are bought and sold. The City of London is a major centre for the massive daily trade in foreign exchange.

Exercises
(20 marks; 25 minutes)

Read the unit, then ask yourself:

1 Give two reasons why the price of a commodity might fall. (2)
2 Are these products commodities or not? Briefly explain your answer.
   a) Galaxy chocolate (3)
   b) large eggs. (3)
3 From the figure on page 154 (Supply and demand for oil in the world market), explain why the price of oil is not $40. (3)
4 Outline two possible causes of a change in worldwide demand for coffee. (4)
5 Look at the figure on page 155 (US $ to the £, 1990–2006).
   a) Describe what happened to the value of the £ between 2002 and 2005. (2)
   b) Explain one possible reason for this change. (3)

Practice questions
(20 marks; 25 minutes)

Oil hits new high on storm fears

World oil prices have hit fresh highs as fears grow over the extent of damage done by Hurricane Katrina to oil output in the Gulf of Mexico.

A barrel of US light crude was trading more than $3 higher at $70.85 early on Tuesday afternoon.

Katrina has shut down 90 per cent of the Gulf's oil output and several refineries, stoking fears about future oil supply. Shell said one of its offshore platforms had been damaged while two of its drilling rigs are adrift in the Gulf of Mexico. Hundreds of other platforms have been closed, reducing output by 1.4 million barrels, equivalent to 7 per cent of US domestic demand.

OPEC – Organization of Petroleum Exporting Countries – is considering raising its production ceiling at a meeting next month. The group, which consists of countries including Saudi Arabia, Iraq, Nigeria and Venezuela, is already busting its limits for daily crude production and has little spare capacity.

Uncertainty

The closure of up to eight refineries and the partial shutdown of a further two has put additional strain on the country's already stretched refining capacity. Fears about the availability of petrol forced wholesale prices to a record $2.85 a gallon on the Gulf Coast.

(Source: adapted from news.bbc.co.uk 30 August 2005)

Questions

1 a) Explain the effect of Hurricane Katrina on the supply and demand for oil. (4)

b) Why did this, in turn, affect the world market price for oil? (3)

2 The oil-exporting countries considering raising production 'next month'. Outline the likely effect of this on the market for oil. (5)

3 Discuss the possible longer-term effect on the motor industry of the shocking rise in the price of petrol at the pumps. (8)

36 Interest rates

The interest rate is the annual percentage charge made for borrowing money. For example, a bank may lend a business £5000 for a three-year period at a rate of 10 per cent. Therefore the business must pay £500 a year in interest, and also repay the £5000. So the borrower pays a total of £1500 for three years' use of £5000.

There are two ways in which this arrangement may cause problems for a business.

1. **When too much money is borrowed**. This is often a problem during a business start-up. The owners put in their life savings of £80,000 and borrow a further £60,000 from the bank. The £6000 a year of interest payments prove higher than the business can afford and within two years it closes down.
2. **When the interest rate rises**. In early 2004 the rate of interest in America was as low as 1 per cent a year. It then went up steadily, reaching 4 per cent by early 2006. A business that borrowed a lot of money in 2004 might struggle to pay four times as much interest as expected, just two years later.

What makes the interest rate rise or fall?

Bank profits come from lending money at a higher interest rate than they pay to get hold of money. Best of all for the banks is when you have money in your current account. They pay you 0 per cent, but use your money to lend to others at perhaps 9 per cent a year. But banks cannot get all the money they want from their customers. Sometimes they need to borrow from the **Bank of England**. Then they have to pay the **bank rate**, which is set every month by an independent committee of the Bank of England. If the bank rate is pushed up, the high-street banks such as Barclays push up the interest rates they charge people or businesses.

Each month the committee decides what rate to set. If the members are worried that the economy may be slowing down, they might cut the bank rate, in order to encourage people and businesses to borrow more and spend more.

What are the effects of lower interest rates?

A cut in interest rates has two main effects on firms:

- more than half of British families have mortgages; a cut in interest rates cuts their monthly payments, leaving them with more spending power; so lower interest rates mean more spending in the shops, especially on luxuries such as leisure, holidays and entertainment. Higher spending means more revenue for businesses, and therefore higher profits (and more jobs)
- lower interest rates mean lower interest charges on firms' borrowings. As most small firms are financed largely through overdrafts, lower interest rates provide an important reduction in fixed overhead costs.

There is therefore a double benefit from lower interest rates: revenues go up and costs go down.

What are the effects of higher interest rates on firms?

Simply, the opposite.

- Households with mortgages need to cut back on spending because they are paying more to the bank/building society.
- Firms have higher fixed overhead costs, which squeezes their profits.
- Both factors may force firms to cut back on investment spending and, perhaps, on staffing.

Do interest rates change much?

In the period 1997–2005 the **Chancellor of the Exchequer** (Gordon Brown) managed the economy very carefully. In this period interest rates were quite stable – and generally falling. The figure below shows clearly how high interest rates have risen in the past.

UK bank rate, June 1985 to January 2006
(source: National Statistics website: www.statistics.gov.uk Crown copyright material is reproduced with the permission of the Controller of HMSO)

In 1989 and 1990 the bank rate reached a high of 15 per cent. It seems extremely unlikely that this will happen again in the next few years, but it should not be ruled out.

Conclusion

Rising interest rates make life hard for all firms, but especially for new, small ones. New firms are likely to have big debts, and are often struggling to make a profit in the early stages. Even business giants such as **Honda** can struggle early on. Honda UK's Swindon factories took more than five years to start making a profit. The combination of large borrowings and low profits is tough on small new firms – especially if the Bank of England starts putting interest rates up.

Revision essentials

Bank of England: the state-owned bank that lends to – and regulates – the high-street banks such as Barclays and Lloyds.

Bank rate: the interest rate set by the Bank of England, from which the high-street banks decide the rates they will charge.

Chancellor of the Exchequer: the government minister responsible for decisions about the economy. The second most powerful politician in the country, after the prime minister.

Exercises

(20 marks; 25 minutes)

Read the unit, then ask yourself:

1. Explain the term 'interest rate' in your own words. (3)
2. Why might an American business that borrowed a lot of money in 2004 struggle when the interest rate rose from 1 to 4 per cent? (4)
3. Briefly explain the likely impact of a sharp rise in interest rates on:
   a) Tesco plc (3)
   b) a car sales business specialising in new Porsche car models (3)
   c) a new restaurant, due to open in three months' time. (3)
4. Business leaders often tell the media they think interest rates should fall. Why are they always likely to want this? (4)

Unit 36 Interest rates

Practice questions

(20 marks; 25 minutes)

Store cards 'need rate warning'

Store card statements should carry warnings to alert consumers to the high interest rates charged by lenders, the Competition Commission has said. If the card's interest rate is higher than 25 per cent then the statement should have a 'wealth warning', the Commission said. Statements should also outline late payment charges and the consequences of only making minimum monthly repayments.

In September the Commission said consumers are being overcharged £100 million a year due to high interest rates. The Commission provisionally concluded that the market for offering consumer credit through retail store cards was uncompetitive.

The body said retailers and lenders were protected from competitive pressures and there was little incentive to reduce annual percentage rates (APRs) on store cards, which currently average about 30 per cent.

Base rate

This compares unfavourably to credit cards, which commonly charge between 15 and 20 per cent, and the Bank of England base rate, which is currently 4.5 per cent.

(Source: www.bbcnews.com/business 21 December 2005)

Questions

1. Why should customers be wary of buying goods with store credit cards costing 30 per cent a year? (4)
2. a) Explain what is meant by the phrase 'protected from competitive pressures'. (4)
   b) At a time when the Bank of England base rate was 4.5 per cent, why might stores be charging an average of 30 per cent on their own credit cards? (4)
3. Discuss whether consumers would act more responsibly with credit cards if there was a 'wealth warning' on any card with an interest rate higher than 25 per cent. (8)

37 Exchange rates

In January 2004 Ted Rahman started importing pink **iPod Minis** from America. He found an American supplier who charged him $225, including delivery to London. With an exchange rate of $1.80 to the £, this meant paying $225/1.80 = £125 per iPod. As the product had not yet been launched in Britain, it was easy to sell these Pink iPods for £200 each. Ted sold 1000 of them in February alone, making an astonishing £75,000.

What Ted noticed was that iPods could be sold in London for £200 while they sold for $225 in America. Yet because the exchange rate allowed him to exchange £1 for $1.80, the price for buying the products in America was just £125. He grabbed the opportunity. By late 2005 iPods were selling in England at much lower prices, and the fall in the value of the £ (to $1.70 per £) made it less attractive to import the products.

What does it mean?

The rate of exchange shows the value of one currency measured by how much it will buy of other currencies. If £1 buys $1.70 in March and $1.75 in April, the £ has risen in value because it buys more $s. The £ is therefore worth more $s.

If the £ buys more $s it makes it cheaper for us to buy American goods. Over the past 15 years the value of the £ has varied from £1= $1 to £1 = $2. If £1 buys $2, then every price you see in an American shop can be halved to work out the British equivalent. For example, a $1 bottle of **Coke** is costing 50p in our money (with $2 to the £, you can buy 2 Cokes for £1).

What changes the exchange value of the £?

The answer is simply supply and demand. If lots of Americans want to buy £s, the high demand for the £ will push up its value (e.g. from $1.70 to $1.75). If lots of British people buy US $s to go on holiday, the price of the $ will rise.

There are many possible causes of higher supply or demand for £s, but the key thing to remember is that it is the balance between supply and demand that determines the price. Demand up, price up; supply up, price down.

Why does a strong £ matter?

It matters because a strong £ (lots of $s to the £) makes it cheaper to import goods from America. This is great for us as consumers because American goods will seem great value. Yet it is tough on British firms that are trying to compete with cheap imports from America. A British shopper is happy if the price of an American computer has fallen from £350 to £290; but a British computer company with production costs of £320 can make a profit at £350, but will make a loss at £290.

So a strong £ is good for British shoppers, but bad for British producers.

The knock-on effects could be even greater. A British producer that cannot compete with American imports may find it has to cut its staffing levels. So British jobs may be lost.

What if the £ is weak?

If the value of the £ is falling against foreign currencies, it is said to be weak. That means the £ buys less of any foreign currency (e.g. £1 used to equal $1.80, but now only buys $1.50). When the £ is weak it costs a British buyer more to buy from overseas. So imports become more expensive, which makes people buy fewer of them. A computer game that sells for $54 in America and used to sell in Britain for $54/$1.80 = £30, is now priced in Britain at $54/$1.50 = £36.

Yet this increase in the price of imports is great for UK producers. Suddenly they find it easier to compete with the higher-priced imported goods. They will also find it far easier to sell overseas, because a weak £ makes our exports better value to foreign buyers.

So a weak £ is bad for British shoppers, but good for British producers.

Other questions about exchange rates

1. **What about the £ against other currencies?** Britain's two biggest foreign markets are Europe and America. Therefore the most important currencies are the euro (€) and the US $. Since it began in 1999, there have usually been about €1.50 to the £. By contrast, there have usually been about 200 Japanese yen to the £.

2. **Can other currencies be worth more than £1?** The answer is yes, they can. Strangely, the £ is worth more than 1 of every other major currency in the world, but that will not necessarily last. If the £ weakened against the US $, it could easily be that £1 might only buy $0.95.

3. **When I go on a foreign holiday, do I want the £ to be high or low?** You definitely want the £ to be strong and therefore allow your £s to buy lots of the foreign currency you need to buy. When £1 gets close to $2, most things seem a bargain to British tourists in America.

Exchange rate calculations

- Rule 1: when exchanging from £s to a foreign currency, MULTIPLY.
- Rule 2: when exchanging from a foreign currency to £s, DIVIDE.

For example, when £1 = $1.80, a £200 **Burberry** jacket should sell in New York for £200 × $1.80 = $360. At the same time, a $900 **Calvin Klein** suit should sell in Britain for $900/$1.80 = £500.

Think: if £1 = €1.40, what price should be charged in Britain for a €21,000 **Audi**?

Conclusion

Companies can be affected greatly by the exchange rate. Manufacturers like the £ to be low so that they can sell goods cheaply overseas and do not face tough competition from imports, as imported goods will be quite expensive. Even more, though, firms like the £ to be stable and therefore predictable in its value. It is hard to trade between America and Britain if the US $'s value is jumping between £1 = $1.20 and £1 = $1.95. This is why some firms have always liked the idea of fixed currency systems such as the euro.

Exercises

(20 marks; 25 minutes)

Read the unit, then ask yourself:

1. What price could be charged in London for $225 iPods when £1 = $1.70? (Answer to the nearest 5p) (3)
2. a) If £1 equalled €1.50 last month, but €1.35 this month, has the £ risen in value or fallen in value? (1)
   b) What would be the effect of this on the export price to Europe of a £200 UK-made coat? (3)
3. Briefly explain why a strong £ is bad for British producers. (4)
4. Outline why a weak £ is bad for British shoppers. (4)
5. Between March 2005 and January 2006 unemployment rose every month. Explain how a falling £ might help to reduce the level of unemployment in the UK. (5)

Practice questions

(20 marks; 20 minutes)

On 1 January 2003 Sean Blake struck his first ever export deal. It was for £20,000 worth of computer software, sold to an Australian bank. As the sales revenue of his whole business had only amounted to £65,000 in 2002, this was a real boost. The only problem was that the £ was very high against the Australian $, making it hard to make a profit on the deal. With the £ valued at Aus$2.85, Sean had to offer a lot of software for the money. In fact, his profit on the £20,000 deal proved to be no more than £450.

Fortunately, the bank was delighted with the software, which helped to keep up-to-date accounts of all the share dealing done by the bank. So when, in January 2006, Sean went to Australia with a brand new, improved piece of software, the bank was very interested. As the £ had fallen to Aus$2.35, he saw the opportunity to make far more profit from the new order. He suggested a price of Aus$70,500 for his new product and was amazed when the bank accepted, without negotiation.

Seeing the opportunity provided by the falling pound, Sean also contacted several other banks in Australia, and found three other buyers. He expects exports to comprise 50 per cent of his 2006/7 turnover of £340,000.

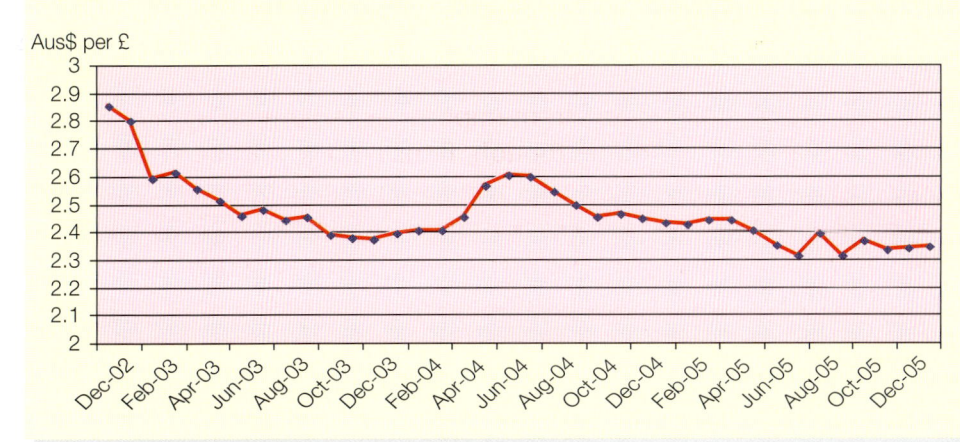

Exchange rate, £ v. Aus$, December 2002 to January 2006)

SECTION 5 Understanding the economic context

Questions

1. When £1 = Aus$2.85 Sean Blake sold £20,000 of software in Australia. What price did he charge in Australian dollars? (2)

2. Why was it so difficult for Sean to make a profit when the £ was high against the Aus$? (5)

3. a) Use the graph to identify the £ to Aus$ exchange rate in July 2004. (1)

   b) At that rate, was the £'s value higher or lower than in December 2002? (1)

   c) Would a British tourist visiting Australia have been better off in December 2002 or July 2004? Briefly explain your answer. (4)

4. a) How much did Sean receive in £s from the January 2006 sale to the Australian bank? (2)

   b) Given the ups and downs of the exchange rate shown in the graph, is Sean right to push for three more sales to Australian banks? (5)

38 Changes in economic activity

A well-run business keeps one step ahead of its competitors. It anticipates changes in customer tastes or buying habits. Therefore it comes up with new products or services just when they are needed. It also makes sure to keep costs under control so that its prices never seem bad value for money. Businesses such as this include **Tesco**, **Primark** and **Toyota**.

Risk of economic downturn

However well-run a business is, it cannot control the economy. In late 1990 the British economy fell back, causing sales to fall month after month for more than two years. Firms that had financed expansion by heavy borrowings could not afford the interest payments – and collapsed. By 1992 high streets were full of closing-down sales and boarded-up shops. In Hatfield, just north of London, a shopping centre on the A1 motorway went into **liquidation** before it had opened up! Worst of all, many families lost their homes because they could not keep up with the mortgage payments.

During a period of recession such as this, falling sales cause job losses that eat away at people's confidence. The threat of unemployment makes people cautious about spending money. Sales of 'big ticket' items are hit especially hard; these include cars, carpets, houses and holidays. Even worse hit are the sales of luxuries such as boats, expensive jewellery and first-class travel.

At the start of 2006, businesses were able to look back on more than 10 years of continuous economic growth, with no **recession** since 1990–92 (see the figure below). Yet good managers will wonder when the next recession will strike and make sure that the business will be capable of surviving it. Above all else, recessions hit firms' cash flow, so it is essential to have enough cash in the bank to cope with difficult times.

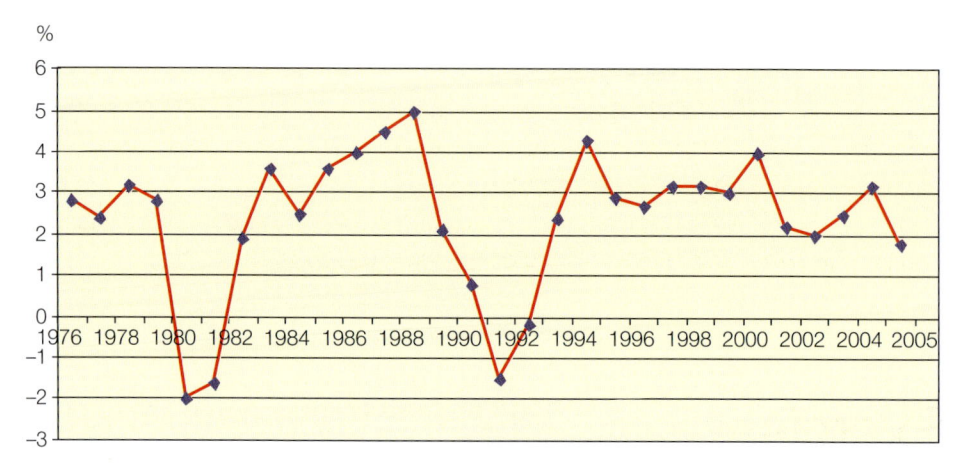

% change in UK economic output, 1976–2005
(source: National Statistics website: www.statistics.gov.uk Crown copyright material is reproduced with the permission of the Controller of HMSO)

Can difficult times be spotted?

There is one clue in the figure above that could help firms to anticipate problems. Before the collapse in output in 1990–92, the economy was **booming**. Between 1984 and 1988 the economy was growing faster each year. In 1988 the economy grew by 5 per cent compared with the previous year. This may not sound a lot, but the British economy usually grows by about 2.5 per cent a year, so 5 per cent was twice the usual rate of growth, and British businesses could not cope. They ran out of factory space, they ran out of staff and the economy ran out of steam.

Overall, the conclusion from this is that recessions often stem directly from boom-times. In other words, if everyone is getting excited that the economy is doing brilliantly, clever businesspeople will start to wonder when and how the boom will end.

Do governments know how to prevent recessions?

In 1997 the new Labour government made the Bank of England responsible for setting interest rates. Since then, it has used this power to dampen the economy down before boom conditions have got out of hand. This seems to have been a great help in preventing recessions. Yet what if a severe recession hits America? The consequences would certainly be severe in Britain. Falling sales in America will hit our exporting companies. This would have knock-on effects throughout the British economy. Therefore it would be silly to think that there will never again be a serious recession in Britain. Governments may think they know how to prevent recessions, but it does not mean that they always succeed.

> **Revision essentials**
> **Booming:** an economy that is growing much faster than it usually does. The term 'boom' implies that it probably will not last (i.e. that the economy is heading for a bit of an explosion).
> **Liquidation:** closing the business down – selling off its assets to raise the cash to pay its debts.
> **Recession:** a downturn in sales and output throughout the economy. The strict definition is 'falling output for two successive quarters of the year' (i.e. for six months in a row).

Exercises

(20 marks; 25 minutes)

Read the unit, then ask yourself:

1 Explain why a discount retailer such as Lidl might cope better with a recession than a luxury goods retailer such as Selfridges. (4)
2 How may consumers behave if they are feeling confident about their future? (3)
3 Look at the figure on page 168 (% change in UK economic output, 1976–2005). Outline one impressive feature and one disappointment in the government's handling of the economy between 1997 and 2005. (4)
4 Examine one approach that could be taken by British Airways to ensure that it does not suffer too severely when the next recession arrives. (4)
5 Explain why governments should try to prevent economic booms from occurring. (5)

Practice questions

(20 marks; 25 minutes)

Steve launched his hi-fi business four years ago. Steve won the contract for selling Bang & Olufsen equipment, selling at prices from £500 up to £8000. At the time, customers and businesses were feeling very optimistic about the economy, so sales were rising sharply. In the run-up to Christmas last year, he sold a £24,000 home cinema and an £8000 music system on the same day!

Steve has been clever to set up his store in the Wirral, where many of the north's best-paid footballers live. They love the unique style of 'B&O' and think nothing of paying half a week's wages for the latest hi-fi equipment. One famous player gave away a six-month-old, £6000 hi-fi to the club's kitman, because he'd just bought a newer model.

Despite this, Steve is aware that only half his sales come from the super-rich; he wonders whether other buyers would keep coming if the economy entered a recession. His first business (a restaurant) collapsed in the 1991 recession, so he does not want to suffer twice over.

Questions

1. Explain two impressive features of the way Steve has set up his business. (4)
2. a) Outline why Steve may be worried about the impact of a recession. (4)
   b) Outline one other problem outside Steve's control that might affect the business. (6)
3. Discuss how Steve might prepare for the possibility of an economic downturn in the future. (6)

39 Forecasting economic activity

Business decisions are all about the future. If you are to open a new restaurant in six months' time, you would love to know the future level of interest rates, consumer confidence and consumer spending. A **forecast** could try to do this. The problem is that economic forecasts may not be accurate.

In February 2006 a famous Cambridge University professor, Wynne Godley, predicted that the American and British economies were vulnerable to a 'prolonged' shortfall in demand. In other words, there could be a severe **recession** lasting a number of years. British and American households had been spending too much and saving too little. Therefore, US and UK consumers were sucking in far too many imports, and needing to cut back their spending to lower their credit card bills.

Reading Professor Godley's predictions might lead any business owner to think hard about risking further expansion. After all, if the economy is due to turn downwards, who would want to spend money to expand a factory or develop new markets?

Yet if you enter 'Wynne Godley' into Google, you quickly find that the professor has been saying very similar things for many, many years. There is an article by him from 2002 which tells a broadly similar story. He may well prove right one day, but accurate forecasting requires getting the timing right.

Quite simply, forecasting the economy is extremely difficult. Therefore every business should take every forecast with a pinch of salt. Forecasts are worth thinking about, and even planning for, but no business should change gear just because of a forecast.

Why bother?

If forecasts cannot be relied on, why do them? Simply because economic changes can be very damaging for firms, so businesspeople need to think about how the future might look. At the time of writing, shop prices in Britain have risen 2 per cent in the past 12 months. Yet the prices factories are paying for their materials have risen 16 per cent in the past year. So the factory owners must be desperate to push their prices up. However, if **Cadbury** put up its prices by 16 per cent, while **Mars** kept to a 2 per cent price rise, Cadbury would lose market share dramatically. Therefore Cadbury has to be able to forecast future consumer price inflation to have a clearer idea about what competitors will do.

Why is it so hard to get right?

One answer is to look at the problems other 'experts' have in forecasting. Every week the BBC website features 'expert' Mark Lawrenson predicting the weekend's football scores. If he gets 3 out of 10 right, the BBC boasts about it! For economists, there are two main problems.

1. It is often hard to be sure what is happening to the economy right now. On any day, some firms moan about tough times on the High Street while others sound positive. This is crucial because if you are not sure whether things are getting better or worse today, it is hard to predict the position in 6 or 12 months' time.
2. There are so many variables that can affect the economy: some are economic variables, such as a rise in the interest rate or the exchange rate; others are human variables, such as rising consumer confidence – 1966 proved a better year for the economy than was expected because consumers felt better about life after England won the world cup!

> 'I'd rather be vaguely right than precisely wrong.'
> J.M. Keynes, world-famous economist

So what should firms do?

The answer is to be prepared. When times are good and consumer spending is rising, it is time to think: what if things turned downwards? Do we have products that people would want or need to buy when times are hard? If the £ is weak against the $ (making exports from Britain very profitable), it is time to ask: what if the £ became stronger? What would we do then?

Well-run firms think ahead. Economic forecasts can help in that process, even if they often turn out to be wrong.

> **Revision essentials**
> **Forecast:** a prediction of the future based on evidence (e.g. forecasting what UK interest rates will be in six months' time).
> **Recession:** a downturn in economic activity (e.g. a fall in consumer spending and therefore in company sales and production).

Exercises

(20 marks; 25 minutes)

Read the unit, then ask yourself:

1 Outline one reason why:
   a) A house-building firm would love to know the interest rate in six months' time. (3)
   b) Honda UK, exporting more than half its output to Europe, would love to know the £/€ exchange rate in six months' time. (4)
2 Briefly explain why it is hard to make accurate economic forecasts. (4)
3 Rolls-Royce luxury cars are made in Sussex, and sell for more than £200,000 each. More than 75 per cent are exported. What might Rolls-Royce do about:
   a) A forecast that interest rates are to rise sharply in the next nine months? (3)
   b) A forecast that the £ is set to fall sharply in the coming weeks? (3)
   c) A forecast that inflation is to rise from around 2 per cent to around 3.5 per cent? (3)

Practice questions

(20 marks; 25 minutes)

Household numbers and projections

	Household numbers (millions)			Household projections (millions)			% increase
	2000	2001	2006	2011	2016	2021	2006–21
North-east	1.09	1.1	1.12	1.14	1.15	1.17	4.50
North-west	2.87	2.88	2.93	3	3.06	3.11	6.10
Yorkshire and the Humber	2.12	2.14	2.2	2.26	2.32	2.37	7.70
East Midlands	1.75	1.76	1.83	1.9	1.97	2.03	10.90
West Midlands	2.18	2.19	2.24	2.3	2.35	2.4	7.10
East	2.28	2.28	2.39	2.49	2.6	2.7	13
London	3.19	3.13	3.25	3.38	3.52	3.65	?
South-east	3.38	3.4	3.57	3.74	3.91	4.06	13.70
South-west	2.1	2.12	2.21	2.32	2.42	2.52	14
England	20.97	20.99	21.73	22.52	23.31	24	?
Wales	1.2	1.21	1.24	1.28	1.31	1.34	8.10

(Source: Office of the Deputy Prime Minister; National Assembly for Wales)

Unit 39 Forecasting economic activity

Questions

1 a) Calculate the forecast percentage increases for London and England as a whole, between 2006 and 2021. Show your workings. (5)

b) Outline two possible effects on Londoners of this increase in the number of households between 2006 and 2021. (4)

2 What business opportunities may there be in England as a result of the increase in the number of households? (5)

3 Discuss the possible impact of the forecast proving inaccurate. (6)

40 Stakeholders

Stakeholders are the people or groups with an interest in the success or failure of an organisation. A business will want to look after those who can help it succeed, which might include the press or the government. These are the **primary stakeholders**. There may also be outsiders who think of themselves as stakeholders, whether or not the organisation wants them to. These are the **secondary stakeholders**. For example, animal rights activists might become concerned at the way a cosmetics business tests new products on animals.

Primary stakeholders

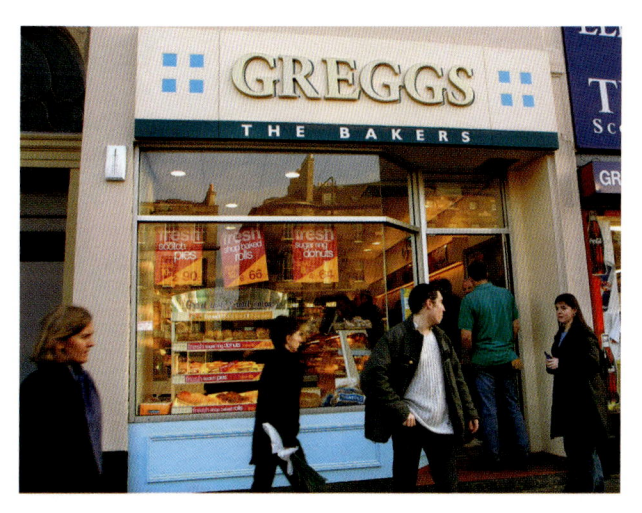

Greggs plc (Britain's biggest chain of bakeries) has always been proud to say that its two key stakeholders are its customers and staff. It places its shareholders in third place, on the grounds that as long as staff and customers are happy, the business will be a financial success. Other companies take a different view. **Cadbury**, for example, declares that its main priority is to maximise returns for its shareholders.

Staff, customers and shareholders are by no means the only stakeholders a business may have to consider. The owner of a good restaurant may consider suppliers to be massively important. S/he may buy steak from a local farmer who produces tender, organic meat. The restaurant's reputation depends on the quality of the farmer's deliveries. Therefore the supplier becomes a primary stakeholder.

For all organisations, the key primary stakeholders are:

- the owners/shareholders
- the staff/managers
- the customers.

In addition, some will also regard suppliers as vital stakeholders.

Secondary stakeholders

Among other possible stakeholders are:

- local residents, who may be affected by traffic noise from deliveries or by pollution from a smelly or smoky factory or farm
- local government, which is the organisation that will give a yes or no to future planning permission; for example, on whether the business is allowed to build a larger warehouse
- pressure groups, such as Greenpeace, who may organise protests if they feel that an organisation's activities damage the environment.

These would all be regarded as secondary stakeholders, though it is possible to imagine that any one of these (or others) may become very important for a particular business. For example, a football club might regard the police as a primary stakeholder.

Organisations and stakeholders

ORGANISATION	OWNERSHIP	3 MOST IMPORTANT STAKEHOLDERS
Manchester United	Family-owned	Supporters Owners Staff
Marks and Spencer plc	Thousands of individual shareholders	Shareholders Customers Staff
Altrincham Bridal Wear Ltd	Family-owned	Customers Suppliers of wedding dresses Shareholders

Small business stakeholders

For most small firms, the keys to success are customers, staff and suppliers. Treating them well and using them well are essential, partly because you never know when you may need them to help you. A really committed restaurant supplier would drop everything and rush to a client that had run out of chicken half way through the evening. A really committed customer may help out when needed (e.g. paying in cash to help a supplier with cash flow problems). Most important of all are the staff, because if they are well motivated, their enthusiasm will rub off onto customers and suppliers.

Are shareholders number one?

The directors of most public limited companies have little choice but to treat shareholders as the most important stakeholder. This is because the shareholders have the right to vote the directors out of office if they believe the business is badly run. Companies such as **Dixons** are open about the priority given to profit and, therefore, shareholder returns. Others prefer to suggest that they treat all stakeholders equally.

British company law sets out that the primary duty of company directors is to the shareholders. This weights the issue clearly in favour of suggesting that most companies will treat the shareholders as the single most important stakeholder.

Conclusion

'He who pays the piper calls the tune.'
Traditional English saying

Companies need to think about their public image. Therefore it is important for managers to think about their wider responsibilities. If they fail to do so, the result might be a bad press, with local residents or national pressure groups making complaints. **Nike** has suffered a bad press in the past from the use of low-cost (even child) labour in making its (very pricey) trainers. Pressure groups (and customers) blamed Nike for ignoring its responsibility to its suppliers.

The issue of stakeholders simply urges firms to think more widely about the effects of their business activities. Well-managed firms have always done this. The risk today is that every firm may claim to care about its stakeholders, whereas day-to-day business decisions may continue to make profit the top priority.

Revision essentials
Primary stakeholders: people or groups seen by the business to be fundamental to the organisation's success or failure.
Secondary stakeholders: people or groups who feel involved in the organisation's success or failure, whether or not the management agrees.

Exercises

(15 marks; 20 minutes)

Read the unit, then ask yourself:

1. Why are employees regarded as primary stakeholders? (2)
2. What is the difference between a shareholder and a stakeholder? (3)
3. Which do you think are the three most important stakeholders for:
   a) your school/college (3)
   b) your nearest sweetshop or grocer's. (3)
4. Outline two possible disadvantages for staff who work for a business that only focuses on the needs of shareholders, not stakeholders. (4)

Practice questions

(20 marks; 25 minutes)

Extract 1: Working with our stakeholders – LloydsTSB

Our customers, shareholders and employees are our key stakeholders.

Customers: understanding our customers' needs and providing products and services that meet these needs is crucial to our business.

Shareholders: we respond to surveys and enquiries from the socially responsible investment indices.

Employees: we include regular features and articles on corporate responsibility issues in our staff magazine.

(Source: extracts from Lloyds Bank's Corporate Responsibility Report 2004, www.lloydstsb.com)

Extract 2: Fifty thousand people who put over £1bn into Lloyds TSB's Extra Income and Growth Plan (EIGP) are being advised not to accept the bank's compensation deal for any losses

The Financial Ombudsman has written to warn investors that if they accept the bank's offer to reimburse them, they could lose out substantially.

The plan – a Scottish Widows product sold by Lloyds TSB between October 2000 and May 2001 – offered a fixed income payout of over 10% a year, or guaranteed growth if the cash was kept invested for the whole three years.

But the capital was at risk, something many people say they were never told.

(Source: BBC Money Box, news.bbc.co.uk)

Questions

1. **a)** Outline what Lloyds Bank says are its responsibilities to its customer stakeholders. (4)
   b) Read extract 2, then decide whether Lloyds Bank is living up to these responsibilities. Explain your answer. (6)
2. Outline one reason why a firm might find it hard to always act in the best interests of its customers. (4)
3. Discuss why a firm such as Lloyds might put its Corporate Responsibility Report on its website, instead of just sending a copy to its staff. (6)

41 The effect of business and economic activity on stakeholders

In 1989 the Ford Motor Company made one of the worst business decisions in history: it paid £1600 million for the Jaguar car business. At the time of the purchase the exchange rate was $1.58 to the £. At that rate, Jaguar could produce cars in Britain and sell them for a good profit in America. Shortly after the purchase went through, the £ rose in value, making it much harder to export profitably to America. Jaguar started losing money. Fifteen years later it was still losing amazing sums. In 2003/4 it lost £600 million and in 2004/5 its losses were nearly £430 million. For Ford, it has been like throwing hundreds of millions down the drain, year after year.

Ford's decision to buy Jaguar was made in the belief that the £ was only likely to get weaker in future against the $. This would have made exporting to America more profitable – and 60 per cent of Jaguars were exported from Britain to America. The fact that the £ strengthened shows how difficult and how important economic factors can be. If Ford knew then what they know now, they would not have paid a penny for Jaguar, let alone £1600 million.

Effect on stakeholders

On employees

Since Ford's purchase, Jaguar has had to cut staffing levels dramatically. In 2004 the closure was announced of its factory in Coventry, with the loss of thousands of jobs in the Midlands. Many factors contributed, but the main ones were the strong £ and an economic slowdown in America. Not only did the Coventry factory closure hit the staff, but also the companies and staff at dozens of small-scale suppliers working close by the Jaguar factory.

On suppliers

Ending production in Coventry will have an immediate effect on many local suppliers of goods and services. The goods might include spark plugs or car tyres – used to manufacture the cars. The services would be from local cleaning and catering companies, taxis and business travel agencies. In addition, local job losses would hit takings at local shops, pubs and clubs.

On shareholders

In 2004 Ford paid out more than $1200 million in interest charges on its bank borrowings. It was lucky that interest rates in America were very low at the time. But rising interest rates – plus the drain caused by Jaguar's losses – led to a 50 per cent drop in Ford's share price in 2005.

Other external factors affecting stakeholders

The term **PEST** is an easy way to remember the political, economic, social and technological factors affecting firms and their stakeholders.

Political factors

Changes made by parliament or government can have a major impact. The Minimum Wage Act came into force in April 1999, setting an adult minimum wage of £3.60 per hour. It became illegal to pay workers less than £3.60 an hour. At the time it meant pay rises for 2 million workers. However, another stakeholder group – the shareholders – may have lost out because higher wages may have been at the cost of lower profits. For October 2006 the rate is £5.35 per hour.

Economic factors

At Christmas 2005 the BBC's economics correspondent said that the two biggest business stories of the year were Google and China. The key story about China was its amazing economic growth, of more than 9 per cent per year. This growth rate has been sustained for more than 10 years, enabling China to go from nowhere to the fourth largest economy in the world in 2006. China's ever growing exports to the West have cost thousands of jobs in British toy, clothing and electronics factories. As consumers, though, we have all benefited from the continually falling prices of products such as shoes and clothes, 'made in China'.

One major impact of China's growth has been on oil prices worldwide. As the graph below shows, China's use of oil (consumption)

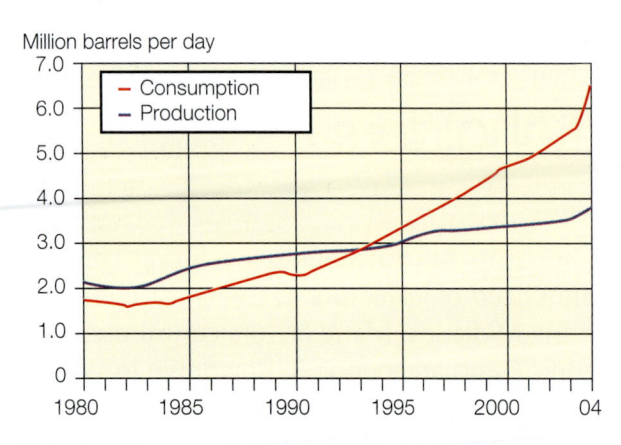

China's oil demand, 1980–2004
(source: Energy Information Administration)

has outstripped its production level. This has made China a huge oil importer. China's demands on the world supply of oil sent prices soaring in 2004 and 2005. This affects every firm and every household. Fortunately, the high prices may force people to be more thoughtful about their use of oil. In America, 'gas-guzzling' trucks are suffering a fall in sales, while the electric Toyota Prius enjoys a sales boom.

Social factors

Two powerful social influences on business are the pressure for healthier lifestyles and the drive to think more about the environment. McDonald's has been dragged down, with sales falling 25 per cent in Britain between 2003 and 2005. This hurts suppliers (cattle farmers, potato processors etc.), employees and shareholders – but hopefully to the advantage of customers, who may be fitter for eating elsewhere. Oil companies have felt under pressure to invest in alternative sources of energy, such as wind and wave power. BP has spent a lot of money advertising its **green** activities. It hopes to benefit its general reputation, thereby making talented graduates willing to work for the company.

Technological factors

The BBC's economics correspondent who said at Christmas 2005 that Google was one of the biggest business stories of the year was referring to the incredibly powerful Google search engine, which was making it ever easier to find the product or the information you wanted at a bargain price. Google was creating new business opportunities, but also making it much harder for some traditional businesses to make a profit.

Conclusion

At the beginning, it is hard to tell the difference between change that is temporary and change that is fundamental. For years people had pointed the finger at the fat content in McDonald's menu, but only in the last few years has it had a serious effect on sales. Stakeholders will only be affected if major changes are taking place. Will Google – as many expect – take on Microsoft and create real competition in computer software? This would affect Microsoft staff (job losses) and suppliers as well as customers. But perhaps Google will choose to avoid tackling super-rich Microsoft head-on. If so, the changes may not look important in the longer term.

Revision essentials

Green: issues about the environment, such as pollution, recycling and sustainability.
PEST: political, economic, social and technological factors that may have an impact on firms.

Exercises

(25 marks; 30 minutes)

Read the unit, then ask yourself:

1 Outline two reasons why Ford should regret having bought Jaguar. (4)
2 Look at the graph on page 180 (China's oil demand, 1980–2004) and identify:
   a) the year when Chinese consumption of oil outstripped the level of production (1)
   b) the approximate gap between consumption and production of oil in 2004. (3)
3 Explain why the gap between Chinese supply and demand for oil would have tended to push up the world oil price. (6)
4 a) Briefly explain your own attitude to eating at McDonald's. (4)
   b) Discuss what McDonald's mangers should do to bring the customers back. (7)

Practice questions

(20 marks; 25 minutes)

Yakult was the originator of the market for 'healthy' yogurt drinks, more than 30 years ago. It was designed to be healthy rather than to taste good. This was also a feature of the advertising, which used the slightly scary claim that the product contained 'good bacteria'.

The market grew steadily but slowly, until the French company Danone entered the market with Actimel. Heavily advertised, and with various sweetened fruit flavours, Actimel was promoted as a fun, enjoyable product rather than a serious one.

At first the advertisements for Actimel helped sales of Yakult, but by 2005 sales started to slip. Consumers wanted the fun, healthy lifestyle promoted by Danone. Also, in 2005, Yakult sales were hit by a new Müller product, Vitality, featuring the 'brain-food' Omega 3. All the clever new products were pushing Yakult to one side.

The bar chart below shows the changes in the sales of these three products in 2005 compared with 2004. They are the top three brands in a market with sales worth £260 million a year.

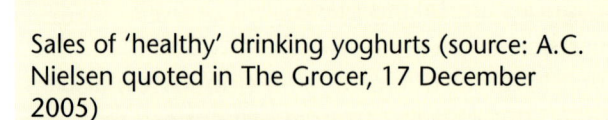

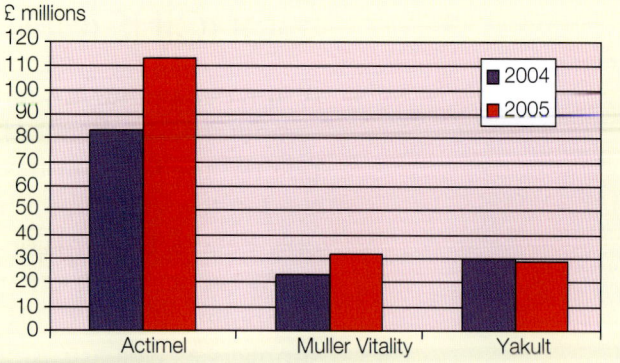

Sales of 'healthy' drinking yoghurts (source: A.C. Nielsen quoted in The Grocer, 17 December 2005)

Questions

1. Outline one good and one bad thing about the determination of Yakult's managers to stick to the product they believe in. (6)
2. Look carefully at the bar chart, then decide whether the following statements are true or false.
   a) Actimel's sales in 2005 grew by more than the total sales of Yakult. (2)
   b) Müller Vitality went from third place in 2004 to second place in 2005. (2)
   c) Actimel's 2005 sales were more than 50 per cent of the total market size of £260 million. (2)
   d) Actimel's sales were £83 million in 2004 and £113 million in 2005, so they rose by 26.5 per cent. (2)
3. Sales of 'healthy' lifestyle products such as these provide big opportunities for large companies such as Danone. Discuss whether companies should be allowed to use advertising to worry people into making purchases. (6)

Tackling the on-screen exam

Unit 1 is the core module of this qualification. Everyone must do it. The exam can be taken at the end of Year 10 and retaken, if necessary, at the end of Year 11.

On-screen exams offer some fantastic benefits to you.

- They make you think, but do not require long answers.
- They give you enough time to answer the questions, and to go back and check each one.
- They put everything you need on the screen in front of you (though you will need a calculator by your side, for the occasional numbers question).
- When you practise them beforehand, the computer can give you immediate feedback, including your marks.

However, there are some specific issues with on-screen exams that you must bear in mind.

- Computer marking means that answers are either right or wrong – there is no halfway; therefore you must be precise. For example, with questions where you type in a one-word answer (e.g. 'exports'), you must check your typing carefully; the computer will be programmed to accept predictable slips (such as 'xports'), but will not know how to recognise 'expkrts', if you hit the wrong key).
- The same point is true of calculations; make sure you check your answers with great care.
- ALL exams require you to focus on the question, but on-screen exams make this essential. If you misread the question in a paper exam, you may waffle your way to half marks. With an on-screen exam a precisely right answer is only possible if have read the question very, very carefully.
- With questions where you are given options, read them all before choosing your answers; it is best to eliminate the weakest answers before selecting the best; make sure you read each answer option with great care.

To sum up, on-screen exams can fool you. Because it is so quick to give an answer (perhaps just one click on a keyboard), there is a temptation to rush. In fact, you need to be slower and more careful than normal. Read everything twice; check everything twice. Right and wrong answers mean more precision and therefore more care.

Summary of key exam techniques

- Read the question *twice* before answering it.
- Check your typing carefully, and check again when you have finished the questions.
- You have more time to think because you have less to write; make sure you use the time effectively.

What next?
Moving on from Unit 1

This GCSE course offers four options for progression. Three provide a single GCSE award; the fourth is a double award (i.e. it is worth two GCSEs).

The three single GCSEs

1   **Business studies.** To achieve the complete GCSE in business studies you need to progress from Unit 1 to Unit 2 (Building a Business). This unit shows how firms grow and develop, detailing the methods and problems involved. It is examined by means of a written exam that tests your ability to write thoughtfully about the subject. Whereas Unit 1 focuses on an entrepreneur starting up a business, Unit 2 looks at the role of managers in creating a larger business organisation. Together they make a complete GCSE business course that is an excellent preparation for A level business studies.

2   **Business and economics.** To achieve the complete GCSE in business and economics you need to progress from Unit 1 to Unit 4 (Introduction to Economics). This unit has a questioning, problem-solving approach to economics. It asks questions such as: What makes people richer? Why belong to the EU? Why do firms go under? It looks at the role of government and Britain's place within the world economy. It is examined by means of a written exam based on your own research. Units 1 and 4 make a complete GCSE business and economics course that provides an excellent preparation for both business studies A level and economics A level.

3   **Business and communications.** To achieve the complete GCSE in business and communications you need to progress from Unit 1 to Unit 3 (Communication Systems). This is a hands-on unit, focusing on how information technology (IT) is used in business. It covers key applications such as spreadsheets, databases and businesslike word processing. It is examined throughout the course,

through classwork exercises completed on the computer. Importantly, this unit forms part of the double-award applied GCSE (see below). So it can be a stepping stone to getting two GCSEs.

The double-award applied business GCSE

Worth two GCSEs, this course consists of Units 1, 3, 5 and 6. Unit 1 is contained within this book and Unit 3 is explained above, so just 5 and 6 need to be set out. Unit 5 focuses on People in Business. It takes you as the starting point, by looking at:

- how to get a (good) job
- how to get on in your career
- what rewards you can expect at work
- what your rights and responsibilities are
- how to manage other people.

The examination is a coursework project, looking at a real-world example of people in business. There is no timed ('external') exam.

Unit 6 covers Change in Business. It includes some calculations, when needed to help make a decision such as: Should Liverpool FC move to a new, bigger stadium? The course content includes:

- causes of change in business, such as economic changes or new competitors
- making decisions to change, using methods such as break-even analysis
- coping with change, including staff resistance to change
- major contexts for change, such as the fashion business or changes in retailing.

The examination is a coursework project, looking at a real-world example of change in business. There is no timed ('external') exam.

The double-award applied business course is excellent preparation for an applied A level course in business studies, or a BTEC National in business or business and finance.

Index

absenteeism 139, 140, 141
Accessorize 53
accountants 117
Actimel 10, 11, 12, 126, 182–3
action, taking 40, 41
Adams, Richard 101
adding value 25–8, 99
    definition 25, 27
    importance of 26–7
    ways to 26
advertising 11
airlines 8, 18, 21, 43, 69–70, 80, 93, 126–7
Aldi 146
Ali, Muhammad 46
AlphaOne Airways 93
amazon.com 7
Andrex 12
annual general meetings 94
Apple 47, 59, 60, 139
Asda 42, 58, 128, 148
assets 94
Audi 164
audiences, target 110, 111
Australian dollar 165–6
availability 10, 11

Bang & Olufsen 169
Bank of England 145, 148, 158–9, 160, 168
bank rate 158–9, 160
banking 6
bankruptcy 116, 118, 119
Barclays 158
Barton, Skye 58
Barton, Ted 58

BASF 20
'being your own boss' 3, 100
Bell, Alexander Graham 29
Bezos, Jeff 7
big business 7
billion 69
bills 84–5
Blair, Tony 62
Bloomsbury Press 56, 57
BMW 49, 145, 149–50
Body Shop 100
Bolan, Adam 136
Bonaparte, Napoleon 61
Boo.com 125
book retail 7
bookkeepers 121
bought-in components 76
brand names 26
Branson, Richard 42, 61, 62, 100, 144
Breeze, Damon 106–7
Brin, Sergey 42
British Airways 8, 18, 21, 70, 80
British Broadcasting Corporation (BBC) 47, 66, 172, 180, 181
British Petroleum (BP) 72, 110, 181
British pound 155, 162, 164
    strong 163, 164
    weak 163
British Retail Consortium (BRC) 148
British Telecom (BT) 18
Burberry 164
Burger King 33, 34, 36
Burton Albion Football Club 138
Bury Football Club 88

INDEX

business failure 51, 54, 67, 90, 96, 116, 167
business growth
    through franchises 34
    and recruitment 132
Business Link 123
business missions 99, 100, 101
business objectives
    financial 99–100
    start-up 99–102
business opportunities
    anticipation of 59
    and cash 85
    spotting 1–37
business organisation
    intelligent 105
    legal issues 121
business ownership 94–5
business plans 4
business problems 59
business strengths 22–4
business success 66–8
business weaknesses 22–4

Cadbury 13, 15, 23, 52, 60, 111, 172, 175
Cafédirect 100–1
Calvin Klein 164
CAP *see* Common Agricultural Policy
capital
    costs of 93
    and delivery 125, 126
    loan capital 95, 96, 97
    share capital 93–4, 97, 116–17
    start-up capital 4, 93–4
    venture capital 95, 97
    working capital 52
car sales 31
cartels 20
cash 84–8, 94, 107
    definition of 86
    importance of 84–5
    management problems 85
    net monthly 89, 91
cash at bank 84
cash flow 87–8
    definition of 86, 89
    negative 90–1
    and recessions 168
cash flow forecasting 89–92
catseyes 44–5

Cauldwell, John 100
Celebrations 12, 15
challenge 139
chance 41
Chancellor of the Exchequer 160
Chanel 110, 111
change
    economic 167–70
    training for 134
charities 40, 100
Chelsea Football Club 10, 150
chemical industry 20
China 180–1
chocolate 15–16, 27–8
choice 7
Cillit Bang 41
clothing 23
clothing materials 153
Coca-Cola 10, 11, 15, 51, 99, 110–11, 162
Codemasters Ltd 45–6, 51
coffee 72
collusion 19, 20
commodities 150, 151, 180–1
commodity markets 153–7
Common Agricultural Policy (CAP) 155
companies
    legal status 121
    limited 116–17, 118, 119, 121
Companies House 116
competition 72
    avoiding head-on 23
    barriers to 19–20
    benefits to consumers 18–19
    drawbacks to 19
    and exchange rates 163
    foreign 146
    local businesses and 23–4
    role and limitations of 18–21
    see also rivals
Competition Commission 161
competitive advantage 127
competitor analysis 22–4
    customer research 22–3
    product/service breakdown 23
    retailer research 23
connection making 59–60
consumers
    behaviour 154
    benefits of competition to 18–19

INDEX

and exchange rates 163
    fashions and tastes of 10, 11
    protection 122
    spending 145, 147, 148
control 53, 116–17
convenience 26
copper 151, 154
corruption 19, 20
costs
    and adding value 26–7
    and cash flow forecasting 89
    cutting 8, 19, 82, 86
    estimating 68, 75–9
    fixed 75–9, 82–3, 159
    and losses 82
    and profit 80, 83
    recording 121
    total 78
    variable 75–9, 82–3
creative thinking 40, 44–6
    deliberate 47–50
credit 86, 91, 96
credit cards 161
Crisby, Philip 3
crisps 75, 76
curriculum vitae (CV) 130, 131
customer focus 104–5, 108–9, 111
customer loyalty 127
customer needs 6–9
    and doing things better 6, 7–8
    and doing things cheaper 6, 8
    and new ideas 6, 7
customer research 22–3
customers
    difficult 113–15
    links with 126
    reliance on only a few 85
    as stakeholders 175, 176, 178, 180, 181
    views of 109
    wants of 52, 59, 108

Danone 10, 11, 12, 30, 126, 182–3
Darling, David 51
Darling, Richard 51
David Lloyd health clubs 147
de Bono, Edward 48, 50
Deal or No Deal (TV quiz show) 47
decision-making 61, 139
Degussa 20

delegation 105
deliberate creativity 47–50
delivery 105, 125–8
    and capital 125, 126
    and management 126
    and physical production capacity 125
    reliable 126–7
    and staff 125, 126
demand 10–14, 71, 125, 149–52
    and availability 10, 11
    balance with supply 150–1
    changes in 154
    and consumer fashions/tastes 10, 11
    effective 10, 12
    and exchange rates 163
    prediction 126
    and price 10–11, 149–51, 153–5, 163
    and promotion 10, 11–12
    and repeat purchases 12
    and sales revenue 71, 72
demand curves 10, 12, 149–50
Deming, W. Edwards 12
design 26
Dillons 61
discrimination 122, 129, 131
Disney, Walt 44
distribution *see* place
dividends 94–5, 97
Dixons 177
Draycott, Ted 71
Drucker, Peter 59, 110
duty of care 113, 114
Dwyer, Karen 98
Dylan, Bob 4
dyslexia 100
Dyson 23, 29, 30, 99, 100

easyInternetcafé 68
easyJet 18, 68
eBay 68
economic booms 168–9
economic context 143–83
    changes in economic activity 167–70
    commodity market prices 153–7
    defining the economy 144–5
    demand 149–50
    economic forecasts 171–4
    exchange rates 162–6
    influences on the economy 145

INDEX

interest rates 158–61
  stakeholders 175–8, 179–83
  supply 150–2
economic downturns 146–7, 167–9
  spotting 168
economic forecasts 171–4
economic growth 145, 154, 156
economic slowdown 144, 145
Einstein, Albert 41, 48
Emerson, R. W. 110
employers 129–31
employment 121–2
  see also staff; unemployment
energy, costs of 76
enterprise 39–63, 126, 1–5
  business trials 3–4
  creative thinking 44–6
  deliberate creativity 47–50
  enterprise skills 40–3
  entrepreneurial qualities 59–63, 3
  reasons for starting a business 3
  risk taking and rewards 51–5
entrepreneurs
  definition of 35
  and franchises 35
  motivation of 138
  qualities of 3, 59–63
environmental issues 31, 122, 181
Eos 70
Esso 110
ethnic minorities 4
EUJet 54, 57
euro 164
European Commission 20
European Union (EU) 145, 155, 156
exchange rates 146, 162–6
  calculation of 164
  influences on 163
excitement 53
exporters 146
exports 145, 147
Extreme Breeze Ltd 106–7

Fairtrade 100–1
Fanta 12
farming 72, 155
  subsidies 19–20
Fat Face 53
Ferguson, Alex 62

Ferrero 23
Fifteen 133–4
finances 52
  intelligent 105
  long-term 94–5
  medium-term 94, 96
  objectives 99–100
  raising 93–8
  short-term 94, 96
  sources of 86
  start-up 66, 68–9, 96
financial records 120–1
fixed costs 75–9, 82–3, 159
Flake 13
flexibility 105, 127
food 153
football 10, 43, 56, 61, 76–7, 88, 100, 138
Ford Motor Company 179–80
forecasts, economic 171–4
foreign exchange markets 155, 156
franchisees 35
franchises 33–7
  benefits of buying 34
  benefits of selling 33–4
  disadvantages of 35
Friends Reunited 103–4
Fulham Football Club 43

games consoles 7–8, 14, 74, 125
garden furniture 66–7
Gates, Bill 42
Geldof, Bob 40
Genes Reunited 105
Girvan, Tamara 120, 121
Glazer family 100
Godley, Wynne 171
Google 42, 180, 181
Goose, Duncan 4, 5, 40
green issues 181
  see also environmental issues
greengrocers 71
Greggs plc 175
Gretsky, Wayne 52

hairdressers 120
Halos n Horns 98
Halstead, Martin 59, 93
Handy, Charles 18
hard work 105

INDEX

Harry Potter 56, 57
Harvard Business Review 53
Hayes, Rutherford 29
Health and Safety at Work Act 114, 121, 122
Health and Safety Executive (HSE) 114
Heinz 72, 110, 151
Herzberg, Professor 135, 138, 139
HM Revenue and Customs 117, 120
HMV 59
Hodgson, Howard 3
Honda 160
Hoover 23
hotels 59–60
house prices 145
HP 72
HSE *see* Health and Safety Executive

IBM 42
Ibuka, Masaru 8
ice cream vans 83
Iceland 131
ideas 6, 7, 48–9
image-building 34
Imperial Chemical Industries 20
importers 146
imports 163
induction 134, 135
Ingham, Sir Bernhard 35
initiative 40, 60, 63
Inland Revenue 120
    see also HM Revenue and Customs
Innocent Drinks 2, 26, 71, 99, 110, 136–7, 152
innovation 30–2
    and competition 18
    definition of 20, 29, 30
    process of 30
    product of 30
interest rates 95, 146, 148, 158–61, 168
    bank rate 158–9, 160
    fixed 95
    high 159
    low 159
    rate of change 160
    rises and falls 158–9
    variable 95, 96
interviews 129, 130
invention 29–30, 45
investment 81, 95, 97, 159

iPod 22, 23, 47, 139
iPod Minis 162
iTunes 59
ITV 103
ITV Digital 88

Jaguar 179–80
Jensens Engineering 141–2
job interviews 129, 130
job skills 130
Jobs, Steve 30
Johnson & Johnson 57
Josephus, Flavius 41

kebab shops 76–8
Kellogg's 110
Keynes, J.M. 172
Kiam, Victor 10
KitKat 7

labour 126
    costing 76, 77
    piece-rate 76
    turnover 140, 141–2
    see also staff
Labour Party 168
Land, Edwin 45
land 126
Lawrenson, Mark 172
leadership 61–2
Leahy, Terry 3, 7, 108
leasing 96
Leaver, Jules 53
legal entities 121, 122
legal issues 120, 121–4
Leighton, Allan 58
Levi's 15
Levitt, Theodore 7, 48
Lexus 26
liability
    limited 105–6, 116–19, 121
    unlimited 116–18
Lidl 146
Lindgren, Robert 25
liquidation 96, 97, 116, 167, 169
liquidators 116, 118
Live8 40
LloydsTSB 178
loan capital 95, 96, 97

local government 176
L'Oréal 30
losses 82
LOT (airline) 21
Lucite 20
luck 105
Lufthansa 126

machinery 76
Magee, William 53
Maltesers 7, 13, 150, 151
management 105
   and delivery 126
   duty of care of 113, 114
Manchester United Football Club 76–7, 100, 138, 176
Mao Tse-Tung 135
market mapping 15–17
market research 7, 15, 16
market segments 23, 24
market share 22, 24
marketing 76
marketing mix 109–12
markets 149, 150, 151
   commodity 153–7
   gaps 52
Marks and Spencer 23, 51, 176
Mars 12, 13, 15, 150, 151, 172
mass production 99
Matalan 23, 146
Mateschitz, Dietrich 54–5
MAXjet 70
McDonald's 33, 34, 35, 36, 51, 181
McGoldrick, P. J. 54
meaningfulness 139
Mercedes 26
metals 151, 153, 154
microbusinesses 6–7
Microsoft 14, 42, 57, 74, 125, 181
milk industry 154
mind maps 60
Mini 7, 49, 145
Minimum Wage Act 122, 180
money
   as commodity 155
   desire for 3
   and motivation 139, 140
monopolies 150, 151
Monroe, Marilyn 61

Monsoon 53
Morrisons 8, 23
mortgages 159
motivation 3, 138–42
Mr Kipling 127
Müller 11, 182–3
music downloads 59
mystery shoppers 109

National Health Service (NHS) 45
National Insurance 122
National Insurance office 117, 120
Nehru, J. 57
Nestlé 48, 57
Newcastle United Football Club 61
Nexus Airlines 43
Nike 26, 41, 177
Nintendo 7–8, 74
Nokia 22, 153
non-profit making organisations 40

Oban Chocolate Company 27–8
objectives, business 99–100, 99–102
Ocado 128
oil 59, 150, 156–7, 180–1
Oliver, Jamie 60, 63, 109, 133
Olsen, William 41
Olympics 2012 59–60
One 4, 5, 40, 100
OPEC (Organization of Petroleum Exporting Countries) 156
opportunities *see* business opportunities
organic produce 102
organisation 105, 121
overdrafts 86, 93, 96
ownership 94–5
Oxfam 100

packaging 11
Page, Larry 42
Paine, Thomas 25
Palmer, Arnold 105
Pankhurst, Julie 103–4
Pankhurst, Steve 103–4
partnerships 117
Patent Office 29
patents 29–30, 100, 101
Patton, General 57
Pepsi 2, 10, 15, 54, 99

personal development training 135
PEST (political, economic, social and technological) factors 180–1
Peters, Tom 134
PG 112
Phones4U 100
piece-rate work 76
Pizza Express 99
Pizza Hut 36, 81
place 109, 110–11
Plato 29
PlayStation 7–8, 14, 74, 125
political issues 180
pressure groups 176
price 28, 109–11
    of commodities 59, 153–7, 180–1
    cutting 8, 19
    and demand 10–11, 149–51, 153–5, 163
    house prices 145
    rivals' 10, 11
    and sales revenue 71–2
    and supply 150–1, 153–5, 163
price competition 15
price fixing 20
price-makers 110
price-takers 110
Primark 23, 167
Pringles 7
printing 50
Prius 31–2
Procter & Gamble 7, 11, 26
product breakdown/analysis 23
product trials 12
production capacity 125
products 72, 109, 110, 111
profit 67
    as business objective 99
    calculation of 80–1, 82–3
    definition of 69, 80
    estimation of 68
    forecasting 80–1
    and price-cutting 8
    reinvestment of 81, 95, 97
    as source of capital 95
promises, delivering on 52
promotion 109, 110, 111
    and demand 10, 11–12
PSP 22, 56, 123
psychometric tests 130

Pureit water purifier 9
purpose, sense of 139

quality 26

Rahman, Ted 162
Ramsay, Gordon 109
raw materials 76
recession 144–7, 167–9, 171
    definition of 173
    prevention 168–9
Reckitt Benckiser 41
Red Bull 54–5
references 130, 131
Reilly, Daniel 43, 59
rent 76, 77, 85
repeat purchases 12
residents 176
restaurants 24, 67–8, 72
    cash flow forecasting 92
    estimating costs 79
    franchises 33–4
    training 133–4
retail 148
retailer research 23
revenue 68
    definition of 69
    estimation of 71–4
    and losses 82
    and profit 80
    see also sales revenue
rewards 51, 53
risk taking 42, 51–5
    calculated 41, 56–8
    main risks 52
    and rewards 51, 53
rivals
    prices 10, 11
    see also competition
Roddick, Anita 100
Rolls-Royce 146
Rollwagen, John 49
Roundabout 5, 40
Rowling, J. K. 56, 57
royalties 35
Ruskin, John 140
Ryanair 8, 69, 127

S&A Foods 42

Safeway 8
Sainsbury's 8, 20, 128
salaries 76
Sale of Goods Act 122
sales forecasts 68, 71, 73
sales revenue 71–4
    calculation 71
    and cash flow forecasting 89
    definition 73
    and demand 71, 72
    and price 71–2
    recording 121
Sam's Brasserie and Bar 24
Samsung 8, 22
Sarnoff, David 19
school dinners 60, 63
Screwfix.com 125
seasonality
    and cash management 85
    and demand 12
selling businesses 53
service breakdown/analysis 23
share capital 93–4, 97, 116–17
shareholders 94–5
    as stakeholders 175, 177, 178, 180
Shaw, Percy 44–5
Shell 110, 156
Sherwood, Dennis 47–9
Simon, Peter 53
Sinatra, Frank 53
Sky TV 7
Skype 68
Slade, Tim 53
Sloan, Alfred 57
Slush Puppy 44
Smith, Adam 19
Snack Wagons 28
social issues 181
social missions 99, 100–1
soft drinks market 17
software companies 45–6
Soil Association 102
sole traders 117, 120, 129
Solero 29
Sony 8, 14, 22, 23, 30, 56, 74, 85, 125, 139
Souness, Graeme 61
Special K 110
spending, consumer 145, 147, 148
staff
    commitment 126
    complacent 58
    and customer focus 108–9
    and customer needs 6–7
    and delivery 125, 126
    and difficult customers 113–15
    duty of care to 113–14
    morale 140
    motivation 138–40
    recruitment 129–32
    as stakeholders 175–6, 178–81
    training 115, 133–7, 139
    turnover 140, 141–2
    see also labour
stakeholders 175–8
    effect of business and economic activity on 179–83
    primary 175, 177
    secondary 175, 176, 177
    small business 176
Starbucks 111
start-up 66–9, 103–42
    and cash flow forecasting 90
    and cash management problems 85
    and customer focus 108–9
    and delivery 125–8
    and difficult customers 113–15
    financing 68–9
    and interest rates 160
    and legal and tax issues 120–4
    and the marketing mix 109–12
    and motivation 138–42
    objectives 99–102
    and over-borrowing 158
    reasons for 3
    and staff recruitment 129–32
    and staff training 133–7
stock exchange 95
stock levels 91
store cards 161
subsidies 19–20
Subway 3, 33, 34, 36–7
success 66–8
Sunny D 152
Superdrug 111
supermarkets
    online business 128
    see also Asda; Sainsbury's; Tesco plc
suppliers

credit 91, 96
payment 85
as stakeholders 175, 176, 180
supply
balance with demand 150–1
changes in 154
and exchange rates 163
and price 150–1, 153–4, 155, 163
supply chain 125–6, 127

takeover bids 95
Tango 12
target audiences 110, 111
taxation 120–1
teamwork 140
technological change 154, 181
Ted Baker 26–7
televisions, flat-screen 8
Tesco plc 3, 7, 8, 11, 20, 42, 71, 72, 98, 108, 114, 126, 128, 135, 167
Tetley 112
thinking ahead 59
Thyme restaurant, London 92
Topshop 23, 76–7
total costs 78
Toyota 31–2, 167
trade credit 96
trade unions 114
Traidcraft 100–1
training 133–7, 139
induction 134, 135
off-the-job 135
on-the-job 135
personal development 135
reasons for 134
Travelodge 147
Trenner, Edgar 129
turnover 121
Twinings 112

unemployment 167
unethical business practices 19, 20, 109, 111
Unilever 9
unique selling points (USPs) 26, 27, 52
unlimited liability 116, 117, 118
US dollar 155, 162, 164

value see adding value
value added tax (VAT) 121
variable costs 75–9, 82–3
venture capital 95, 97
Virgin 42, 144
Virgin Atlantic 70
vision 104, 106
Voltaire 130

wages
ability to pay 84–5, 86
and motivation 139, 140
Walkers 25, 75, 76, 152
Walkers TV, Radio and Music Centre Ltd 115
Walls ice cream 11, 29
Warsi, Perween 42
water
bottled 4, 5, 40, 100
safe drinking 9
Waterstones 61
Weakest Link, The (TV quiz show) 47
wealth 53
weather 12
webdesign 50
Wheeling, Gordon 131
Whitbread 147
Who Wants to be a Millionaire? (TV quiz show) 47
wholesale 150, 151
'Why?', asking 44
'Why not?', asking 44–5
Wilcox, Leila 98
Williams, Robbie 72
Wizz Air 21
women 4
word of mouth 103, 106
working capital 52
Working Time Directive 122
World Health Organization (WHO) 9
Wrangler 15

Xbox 14
Xbox 360 74, 125

Yakult 182–3

Zara 23